Mary Ellen's
BEST
OF HELPFUL HINTS

Mary Ellen's BEST OF HELPFUL HINTS

Mary Ellen Pinkham
and
Pearl Higginbotham

Illustrations by
Lynn Johnston

NEW ENGLISH LIBRARY/TIMES MIRROR

Dedication

This book
is dedicated to our many friends
who made this
collection of helpful hints
possible

Acknowledgements

The authors wish to express their appreciation to
Courage Center Auxiliary, Southwest Lioness Club,
Sheila 'Mouse' Doar, Irene Rice, Wilbur Toll, June
Mattson, Metro Marketing, Gen Bolger, Bruce
Lansky and Associates.

*You've all played a big part in making The Best of
Helpful Hints a bestseller.*

Introduction to the American edition

If you've heard a lot of 'helpful hints' but can't remember them when you've got red wine all over your best tablecloth or stains on the new carpet, then this book was designed for you. We've read (and tested) hints from literally hundreds of sources, discarded most of them and collected only the very best. We've organised them into convenient categories for quick references when you really need them.

Our hints are easy to use and employ items usually found in most kitchen cupboards or workshop shelves. Others use items readily available from your neighbourhood drug or hardware store. Few require expensive commercial cleaning products.

That's not to imply, of course, that our hints are restricted to cleaning. Valuable tips on plant care, beauty aids, childraising, cooking and many more are included. In short, anything to make your life a bit easier and a bit more fun.

We've even supplied a few blank pages at the end so you can write down the next helpful hint that sounds good to you and add to what might well be your most useful and most used reference book.

the BEST of hints for

the BEST
of hints for
THE
KITCHEN

Oops!
When something
goes wrong

Too salty
- For soup and stew, add cut-up raw potatoes and discard once they have cooked and absorbed the salt.
- Another remedy for salty soup and stew is to add a teaspoon each of cider vinegar and sugar.
- Or, simply add sugar.

Too sweet
- Add salt.
- If it's a main dish or vegetable, add a teaspoon of cider vinegar.

Pale gravy
- Colour with a few drops of gravy browning.
- To avoid the problem in the first place, brown the flour well before adding the liquid. This also helps prevent lumpy gravy.
- A different way of browning flour is to put some flour into an ovenproof bowl or dish and place beside meat in the oven. Once the meat is done the flour will be nice and brown, ready to make a rich, brown gravy.

Thin gravy

- Mix water and flour or cornflour into a smooth paste. Add gradually to the gravy stirring constantly, and bring to a boil.
- Try instant potato flakes instead of flour.

Gravy—smooth as silk

- Keep a jar with a mixture of equal parts of flour and cornflour. Put 3 or 4 tablespoons of this mixture in another jar and add some water. Shake, and in a few minutes you will have a smooth paste for gravy.

Greasy gravy

- Add a small amount of bicarbonate of soda if it is quite greasy.
- See Removing the Excess Fat, Kitchen Hints.

Wilted vegetables

- If fresh vegetables are wilted or blemished, pick off the brown edges. Sprinkle with cool water, wrap in towel and refrigerate for an hour or so.
- Perk up soggy lettuce by adding lemon juice to a bowl of cold water and soak for an hour in the refrigerator.
- Douse quickly in hot and then ice water with a little apple cider vinegar added.
- Lettuce and celery will crisp up fast if you place it in a pan of cold water and add a few raw sliced potatoes.

Cream that will not whip

- Chill cream, bowl and beater well.
- Set bowl of cream into a bowl of ice while you're whipping.
- Add the white of an egg. Chill and then whip.
- If the cream still does not stiffen, gradually whip in 3 or 4 drops of lemon juice.
- Cream whipped ahead of time will not separate if you

add a touch of unflavoured gelatin ($\frac{1}{4}$ teaspoon per cup of cream).

- To eliminate a lot of mess when whipping cream with an electric beater, try this: Cut 2 small holes in the middle of a piece of waxed paper, then slip the stems of the beaters through the holes and attach the beaters to the machine. Simply place paper and beaters over the bowl and whip away.

Soggy mashed potatoes
- Overcooked potatoes can become soggy when the milk is added. Sprinkle with dry powdered milk for the fluffiest mashed potatoes ever.

Soggy potato crisps, cereal and water biscuits
- If potato crisps lose their freshness, place under the grill for a few moments. Care must be taken not to brown them.
- You can crisp soggy cereal and water biscuits by putting them on a baking sheet and heating for a few minutes in the oven.

Brown sugar 'hard as a rock'
- If you need it in a hurry, simply grate the amount called for with a hand grater.
- Soften by placing a slice of soft bread in the package and closing tightly. In a couple hours the brown sugar will be soft again.
- Put brown sugar and a cup of water (do not add to the sugar, set it alongside it) in a covered pan. Place in the oven (low heat) for a while.

Frozen bread loaves and rolls
- Place in brown paper bag and put in 325-degree oven (Gas Mark 3) for 5 minutes to thaw completely.

To keep the salt shaking

- Wrap a small piece of aluminium foil tightly around the shaker. The foil is moisture proof and it will keep dampness out of the salt.
- To prevent clogging, keep 5 to 10 grains of rice inside your shaker.

Hurry ups
getting it done in the shortest time possible

Baked potatoes in a hurry
- Boil them in salted water for about 10 minutes before popping into a very hot oven.
- Cut a thin slice from each end before popping into the oven.
- Insert a nail to shorten the baking time by 15 minutes.

Chopping onions without tears
- You'll shed fewer tears if you cut the root end of the onion off last.
- Freeze or refrigerate before chopping.
- Peel under cold running water.
- Or, periodically rinse hands under cold water while chopping.

Peeling thin-skinned fruit
- Refrigerate tomatoes. Hold tomato firmly and scrape with a paring knife from the bottom to the top several times. Prick the skin with the point of the knife. The peel will remove easily.
- Place thin-skinned fruits in a bowl, cover with boiling water and allow to stand for 1 minute. Peel with a paring knife.
- Or, spear the fruit on a fork and hold over a gas flame until the skin cracks, then peel.

Ripe ideas

- Place green fruits in a perforated plastic bag. The holes allow air movement, yet retain the odourless ethylene gas which fruits produce to promote ripening.
- Exposure to direct sunlight softens tomatoes instead of ripening them. Leave the tomatoes, stem-up, in any spot where they will be out of direct sunlight.
- Ripen green bananas or green tomatoes by wrapping them in a wet dish towel and placing them in a paper sack.
- Bury avocados in a bowl of flour.

Removing the excess fat

- If time allows, the best method is refrigeration until the fat hardens on the top.
- Eliminate fat from soup and stew by dropping ice cubes into the pan. As you stir, the fat will cling to the cubes. Discard the cubes before they melt. Or, wrap ice cubes in a piece of cheesecloth or paper towel and skim over the top.
- Lettuce leaves absorb fat also. Place a few into the pan and watch the fat cling to them.
- If you prop up one leg of your electric fry-pan (set it on a knife handle) you can make relatively grease free hamburgers or bacon by frying on the elevated side of the pan.
- When grilling meat on a rack, place a piece of bread in the grill pan to soak up the dripping fat. This not only eliminates smoking fat, but reduces the chances of the fat catching fire.

Eliminating the spattering and sticking

- When frying or sauteeing, always heat your pan before adding the butter or oil. Not even eggs stick with this method.

- Sprinkle a little salt into the frying pan to prevent spattering.
- Vinegar brought to a boil in a new frying pan will prevent foods from sticking.
- When frying, turn a metal colander upside down over the frying pan. This allows steam to escape, but keeps the fat from spattering.
- Meat loaf will not stick if you place a slice of bacon on the bottom of the pan.

Banishing unpleasant cooking smells

- While cooking vegetables that give off unpleasant smells, simmer a small pan of vinegar on top of the stove.
- Or, add vinegar to the cooking water.
- Add a few teaspoons of sugar and cinnamon to an empty baking tin and slowly burn over the stove. Your family will think you have been baking all day.

Tenderising meat

- *Boiled meat:* Add a tablespoon of vinegar to the cooking water.
- *Tough meat or game:* Make a marinade of equal parts cooking vinegar and heated bouillon. Marinade for two hours.
- *Steak:* Simply rub in a mixture of cooking vinegar and oil. Allow to stand for 2 hours.
- And if you want to stew an old hen, soak it in vinegar for several hours before cooking. It will taste like a spring chicken!

Don't 'clam up'

- Shellfish will be simple to open if washed with cold water, then placed in a plastic bag and put in the freezer for an hour.

Preventing boil-overs

- Add a lump of butter or a few teaspoons of cooking oil to the water. Rice, noodles or spaghetti will not boil over or stick together.

Preventing skin on sauces and jellies

- Spread a thin layer of melted butter or cream over jellies, puddings and other sauces right after cooking. Stir and all the skin and foam will disappear.

Preparing cut fruit ahead of time
- Toss the freshly cut fruit in lemon juice and it will not darken. The juice of half a lemon is enough for a quart or two of cut fruits.
- Or, cover with 1 cup syrup made of equal parts of water and sugar cooked until syrupy.

Softening butter
- Grating a block of butter which is hard from the fridge softens it quickly.
- Soften for spreading by inverting a small heated pan over the butter dish for a while.

Measuring sticky liquids
- Before measuring honey or other syrup, oil the cup with cooking oil and rinse in hot water.

Instant white sauce
- Blend together 1 cup soft butter and 1 cup flour. Spread in an ice cube tray, chill well, cut into 16 cubes before storing in a plastic bag in the freezer. For medium-thick sauce, drop 1 cube into 1 cup of milk and heat slowly, stirring as it thickens.

Getting the sauce or ketchup out of the bottle
- Insert a drinking straw, push it to the bottom of the bottle, and then remove. Enough air will be admitted to start an even flow.

Unmoulding the jelly
- Rinse the jelly mould in cold water and then coat with salad oil. Your jelly will drop out easily and will have an appealing lustre.

Hamburgers in a hurry
- Poke a hole in their centres when shaping. The centre will cook quickly and when the hamburgers are done, the holes are gone.

Shrinkless sausage
- Sausages will shrink less and not break at all if they are boiled about 8 minutes before being fried.
- Or, you can roll them lightly in flour before frying.

Removing the silk from sweet corn
- Dampen a paper towel or terry cloth and brush downward on the cob of corn. Every strand should come off.

Cutting sticky foods
- Before chopping, flour the pieces in a paper bag.
- Or, dip your scissors or knife in hot water while cutting.

What a ham!
- Ridding the ham of the rind: Slit the rind lengthwise on the underside before placing it in the roasting pan. As the ham bakes, the rind will pull away and can be removed easily without lifting the ham.

A good cup of coffee

- One pinch of salt in the basket will remove some of the acid taste. For clear coffee, put egg shells in after perking. And remember, always start with cold water.

Your own mini 'Mr Coffee'

- Put a teaspoon of 'drip' coffee into a small strainer ($2\frac{1}{2}$ inch diameter) and place in a cup. Pour boiling water over grounds until cup is full. Steep to desired strength. It's not a bad idea to place mini coffee filters (make your own) in the strainer before adding coffee.

Two 'flavourite' hints

- A different flavouring for tea: Instead of using sugar, dissolve old-fashioned lemon drops or hard mint candy in your tea. They melt quickly and keep the tea clean and brisk.
- Iced tea: Add a small amount of very hot water to instant tea before adding cold water. The crystals will dissolve completely for better flavour.

Some 'nutty ideas'
for shelling

Shelling Brazil nuts
- Bake at 350 degrees for 15 minutes, or freeze. Crack and shell.

Shelling chestnuts
- Cut a slit in the flat side of each nut; cover with water; boil for 10 minutes. Use a paring knife to peel off shell, then membrane.

Shelling walnuts
- If it's important to get the walnut meat out whole, soak the nuts overnight in salt water before cracking gently.

Opening coconuts
- Puncture the eyes with a sharp skewer and drain out the coconut milk. Place the coconut in a shallow pan and

bake at 350 degrees for 45 minutes to 1 hour, until the shell begins to crack. Cool it enough to handle, then tap it smartly with a hammer. The shell will almost spring apart. Pry out the meat with a knife.

Shredding coconuts

- Peel off brown skin with a swivel-bladed peeler or paring knife. Place pieces of coconut in blender with some of the coconut milk (or the liquid called for in the recipe). Process until fine; pour out and continue with the remaining coconut. This short-shredded coconut is suitable for use in pie fillings, batters and fruit deserts.

How to prepare a hard-boiled egg

- Don't laugh, there is more to it than you think. Place eggs in a pan, cover with cold water and pour in some vinegar or salt. The vinegar will keep the eggs from

23

oozing out if the shells crack while cooking. Bring to a boil and remove from heat. Leave to stand in covered pan for 15 minutes. Drain off hot water. Now shake the pan back and forth, causing the eggs to crack against the side. Cool with cold water and peel.

Here are some more 'eggscellent' hints

- To determine whether an egg is fresh without breaking the shell, immerse the egg in a pan of cool salted water. If it sinks to the bottom, it is fresh. If it rises to the surface, throw it away.
- Fresh eggs are rough and chalky in appearance. Old eggs are smooth and shiny.
- To determine whether an egg is hard-boiled, spin it. If it spins round and round, it is hard-boiled. If it wobbles and will not spin, it is raw.
- Pierce the end of an egg with a pin, and it will not break when placed in boiling water.
- A few drops of vinegar will keep poached eggs from running all over the pan.
- Eggs beat up fluffier when not too cold. They should be at cool room temperature for best results.
- By adding vinegar to the water, you can boil cracked eggs without having the white run out of the shell.

- When eggs are stuck to the carton, just wet the box and the eggs can be easily removed without cracking the shells.
- Beaten egg whites will be more stable if you add 1 teaspoon cream of tartar to each cup of egg whites (7 or 8 eggs).
- A small funnel is handy for separating egg whites from yolks. Open the egg over the funnel and the white will run through and the yolk will remain.
- For baking, it's best to use medium to large eggs. Extra large eggs may cause cakes to fall when cooled.
- Brown and white shelled eggs are of the same quality.
- Egg shells can be removed easily from hot hard-boiled eggs if they are quickly rinsed in cold water first.
- To keep egg yolks fresh for several days cover them with cold water and store in the refrigerator.
- Egg whites can be kept frozen up to 1 year. Add them to a plastic container as you collect them, for use in meringues. 1 cup equals 7 or 8 egg whites. You can also refreeze defrosted egg whites.
- For fluffier omelets, add a pinch of cornflour before beating.

Cleanups—
for 'all around' the kitchen

Appliances
- To rid yellowing from white appliances try this: Mix together: $\frac{1}{2}$ cup bleach, $\frac{1}{4}$ cup bicarbonate of soda and 4 cups warm water. Apply with a sponge and leave for 10 minutes. Rinse and dry thoroughly.
- Instead of using commercial waxes, shine with surgical spirit.
- For quick clean-ups, rub with equal parts water and household ammonia.
- Or, try soda water. It cleans and polishes at the same time.

Baking tins
- Remove rust by dipping a raw potato in cleaning powder and scouring.

Blender
- Fill part way with hot water and add a drop of detergent. Cover and turn it on for a few seconds. Rinse and drain dry.

Burnt and scorched pans
- Sprinkle burnt pots liberally with bicarbonate of soda, adding just enough water to moisten. Leave to stand for several hours. You can generally lift the burned portion right out of the pan.
- Stubborn stains on non-stick cookware can be removed

by boiling 2 tablespoons of bicarbonate of soda, $\frac{1}{2}$ cup vinegar and 1 cup water for 10 minutes. Re-season pan with salad oil.
- Always place a jar lid or marbles in the bottom part of your double boiler. The rattling sound will signal if the water has boiled away.
- See Grill pan, Kitchen Hints.

Cast iron pans
- Clean the *outside* of the pan with commercial oven cleaner. Leave for 2 hours and the accumulated black stains can be removed with vinegar and water.
- After cleaning pan, take a piece of waxed paper and while pan is still warm, wipe around the inside to prevent rusting.
- Or, when clean rub a small amount of oil on the inside of the pan to keep it seasoned.

Chopping boards
- To rid chopping board of onion, garlic or fish smell, cut

27

a lime or lemon in two and rub the surface with the cut side of the fruit.
- Or, make a paste of bicarbonate of soda and water and apply generously. Rinse.

Copper pots
- Fill a spray bottle with vinegar and add 3 tablespoons of salt. Spray solution liberally on copper pot. Leave for a while, then simply rub clean.
- Dip lemon halves in salt and rub.
- Or, rub with Worcestershire sauce or ketchup. The tarnish will disappear.

Dishes
- Save time and money by using the cheapest brand of dishwashing detergent available, but add a few table-spoons of vinegar to the dishwater. The vinegar will cut the grease and leave your dishes sparkling clean.
- Before washing fine china and crystal, place a towel on the bottom of the sink to act as a cushion.
- To remove coffee or tea stains and cigarette burns from fine china, rub with a damp cloth dipped in bicarbonate of soda.
- To quickly remove food that is stuck to a casserole dish, fill with boiling water and add 2 tablespoons of bicarbonate of soda or salt.

Dishwasher film
- Fill dishwasher with all your dirty dishes. However, never put any silver, aluminium or brass in the washer when this method is used or you will have a mess. Put a bowl in the bottom of the dishwasher. Pour 1 cup of household bleach into the bowl. Run through washing cycle but do not dry. This is important. Fill bowl again with 1 cup of white vinegar and let the dishwasher go through entire cycle. This will remove all film not only from your glasses but from your dishwasher too.

Drains

- When a drain is clogged with grease, pour a cup of salt and a cup of soda into the drain followed by a kettle of boiling water. The grease will usually dissolve immediately and open the drain.
- Coffee grounds are a no-no. They do a nice job of clogging, especially if they get mixed with grease.

Garbage disposal

- Grind a half lemon or orange rinds in the disposal to remove any unpleasant smells.

Glassware

- Never put a delicate glass in hot water bottom side first; it will crack from sudden expansion. The most delicate glassware will be safe if it is slipped in edgewise.
- Vinegar is a must when washing crystal. Rinse in 1 part vinegar to 3 parts water. Air dry.
- When one glass is stuck inside another, do not force them apart. Fill the top glass with cold water and dip the lower one in hot water. They will come apart without breaking.
- A small nick in the rim of a glass can be smoothed out by using an emery board.
- Scratches on glassware will disappear if polished with toothpaste.

Grill pan

- Sprinkle the hot pan heavily with dry laundry detergent. Cover with a dampened paper towel and let the burned food set for a while. The pan should require little scouring.

Grater

- For a fast and simple clean-up, rub salad oil on the grater before using.
- Use a toothbrush to brush lemon rind, cheese, onion or whatever out of the grater before washing it.

Kettle

- To remove lime deposits, fill with equal parts vinegar and water. Bring to the boil and allow to stand overnight.

Mincing machine

- Before washing, run a piece of bread through it.

Oven

- Following a spill, sprinkle with salt immediately. When oven is cool brush off burnt food and wipe with a damp sponge.
- Sprinkle bottom of oven with automatic dishwasher soap and cover with wet paper towels. Leave to stand for a few hours.
- A quick way to clean oven parts is to place a bath towel in the bath and pile all removable parts from the oven on to it. Run enough hot water to just cover the parts and sprinkle a cup of dishwasher soap over it. While you are cleaning the inside of the oven, the rest will be cleansing itself.
- An inexpensive oven cleaner: Set oven on warm for about 20 minutes, then turn off. Place a small dish of full strength ammonia on the top shelf. Put a large pan of boiling water on the bottom shelf and leave it overnight. In the morning, open oven and let it air a while before washing off with soap and water. Even the hard baked-on grease will wash off easily.

Plastic cups, dishes and containers

- Coffee or tea stains can be scoured out with bicarbonate of soda.
- Or, fill the stained cup with hot water and drop in a few denture cleanser tablets. Leave to soak for 1 hour.
- To clear unpleasant smells from plastic containers, place crumpled-up newspaper (black and white only) in the container. Cover tightly and leave overnight.

Refrigerator

- To help eliminate smells fill a small bowl with charcoal (the kind used for potted plants) and place it on a shelf in the refrigerator. It absorbs odours rapidly.
- An open box of bicarbonate of soda will absorb food smells for at least a month or two.
- A little vanilla poured on a piece of cottonwool and placed in the refrigerator will eliminate smells.
- To prevent mildew from forming, wipe with vinegar. The acid effectively kills the mildew fungus
- Use a glycerine-soaked cloth to wipe sides and shelves. Future spills wipe up more easily. And after the freezer has been defrosted, coat the inside coils with glycerine. The next time you defrost, the ice will loosen quickly and drop off in sheets.

Sinks

- For a sparkling white sink, place paper towels across the bottom of your sink and saturate with household bleach. Leave for $\frac{1}{2}$ hour or so.
- Rub stainless steel sinks with lighter fluid if rust marks appear. After the rust disappears, wipe with your regular kitchen cleaner.
- Use a cloth dampened with surgical spirit to remove water spots from stainless steel.
- Spots on stainless steel can also be removed with white vinegar.
- Soda water will shine up stainless steel in a jiffy.
- See Bathroom cleaners, Bathroom Hints

Sponge

- To renew and freshen, soak overnight in salt or bicarbonate of soda water.
- Wash in dishwasher.

Thermos flask

- Put a few tablespoons of bicarbonate of soda in the flask and fill with warm water.

- Or, drop in a few denture cleanser tablets and let soak for an hour or so.

Tin opener
- Loosen grime by brushing with an old toothbrush. To clean blades thoroughly, run a paper towel through the cutting process.

Keeping food fresh
and other kitchen goodies

Bacon and sausage
- To prevent bacon from curling, dip the strips in cold water before frying.
- Bacon will lie flat in the pan if you prick it thoroughly with a fork as it fries.
- Keep bacon slices from sticking together; roll the package into a tube shape and secure with rubber bands.
- A quick way to separate frozen bacon: Heat a spatula over the stove burner, then slide it under each slice to separate it from the others.
- Have you ever tried to get roll sausage out of a package, only to find that half of it is stuck to the surrounding paper? Try running cold water over the paper before you remove the contents. Or, let it stand in ice cold water for a while.

Bananas
- Toss freshly peeled bananas in lemon juice and they will not darken.
- Freeze bananas that are on the verge of going bad. They also make delicious ice lollies.
- If they've darkened, peel and beat slightly. Put into a plastic container and freeze until it's time to bake bread or cake.

Biscuits
- Place crushed tissue paper on the bottom of your biscuit tin.

3

- Can be kept crisp in the most humid weather by storing in the refrigerator. Be sure they are wrapped securely.

Bread
- A rib of celery in your bread bag will keep the bread fresh for a longer time.
- Freshen dried bread by wrapping in a damp towel and placing it in the refrigerator for 24 hours. Remove towel and heat bread in oven for a few minutes.

Broccoli
- Broccoli stems can be cooked in the same length of time as the flowers if you make X incisions from top to bottom through stems.

Brown sugar
- Store in plastic bag. Wrap tightly. Place in coffee tin with snap-on lid.

Butter
- A butter stretcher: To make 2 pounds of butter, slowly beat in 2 cups of evaporated milk (a little at a time) to 1 pound of butter. Pour into a loaf tin and chill.

Cake
- Place $\frac{1}{2}$ apple in the cake box.
- Or, a slice of fresh bread fastened with toothpicks to the cut edge of a cake will keep the cake from drying out and getting stale.

Cheese
- To keep cheese from drying out, wrap in a cloth dampened with vinegar.

34

Corn
- To keep sweet corn yellow add 1 teaspoon lemon juice to the cooking water, a minute before you remove it from the stove.
- Salted cooking water only toughens corn.

Cottage cheese
- Store carton upside down. It will keep twice as long.

Fish and prawns
- Thaw fish in milk. The milk draws out the frozen taste and gives a fresh-caught flavour.
- Or, try soaking fish in vinegar and water before cooking it for a sweet tender taste.
- The fishy smell can be removed from your hands by washing with vinegar and water or salt and water.
- To get rid of the 'tinned taste' in tinned prawns, soak them in a little sherry and 2 tablespoons of vinegar for about 15 minutes.

Garlic
- Garlic cloves can be kept in the freezer. When ready to use, peel and chop before thawing.
- Or, garlic cloves will never dry out if you store them in a bottle of cooking oil. After the garlic is used up, you can use the garlic-flavoured oil for salad dressing.

Honey
- Put honey in small plastic freezer containers to prevent granulating. It also thaws out in a short time.
- If it has sugared, simply place the jar in a boiling pot of water.

Ice cream
- Ice cream that has been opened and returned to the freezer sometimes forms a waxlike film on the top. To

prevent this, after part of the ice cream has been removed press a piece of waxed paper against the surface and reseal the carton.

Lemons

- Store whole lemons in a tightly sealed jar of water in the refrigerator. They will yield much more juice than when first purchased.
- After you've squeezed a lemon for its juice, wrap and freeze the rind. When a recipe calls for lemon rind, you will not have to grate a fresh lemon.
- Submerging a lemon in hot water for 15 minutes before squeezing will yield almost twice the amount of juice.
- Or, warm the lemon in your oven for a few minutes before squeezing.

Lettuce and celery

- They keep longer if you store them in the refrigerator in paper bags instead of cellophane ones. Do not remove the outside leaves of either until ready to use.
- Lettuce will not rust as quickly if you place a paper towel or napkin in the storage container.
- Line the bottom of the vegetable compartment with paper towelling. This absorbs the excess moisture and keeps all vegetables and fruits fresher for a longer period of time.
- Or, put a few dry sponges in the vegetable compartment to absorb moisture.

Meat

- When browning any piece of meat, the job will be done more quickly and effectively if the meat is perfectly dry and the fat is very hot.

Olive oil

- You can lengthen the life of olive oil by adding a cube of sugar to the bottle.

Onions
- Once an onion has been cut in half, rub the left-over side with butter and it will keep fresh longer.

Parsley
- Keep fresh and crisp by storing in a wide-mouth jar with a tight lid.
- Parsley can also be frozen.

Too many peeled potatoes
- Cover them with cold water to which a few drops of vinegar have been added. Keep refrigerated and they will last for 3 or 4 days.

Potatoes

- A leftover baked potato can be rebaked if you dip it in water and bake in a 350-degree oven for about 20 minutes.

Poultry

- After flouring chicken, chill for 1 hour. The coating adheres better during frying.
- For golden brown chicken every time, put a few drops of yellow food colouring in the fat before it has heated.
- Wear rubber gloves to transfer a roast bird from roasting tin to dish.
- Truss the bird with dental floss when grilling. Dental floss does not burn and is very strong.

Salad

- To remove the core from a head of lettuce, hit the core end once against the countertop sharply. The core will then twist out. This method prevents unsightly brown spots which result when you cut into the core end.

- If salad greens are wet and you need them right away, place in a pillow case and spin dry in your washing machine for a few seconds. This hint is especially good to know if you are serving salad to a large crowd.

Salt

- Since most recipes call for both salt and pepper, keep a large shaker filled with a mixture of both. $\frac{3}{4}$ salt and $\frac{1}{4}$ pepper is a good combination.
- When to add salt:
    Soup and stews: Add early.
    Meats: Sprinkle just before taking off the stove.
    Vegetables: Cook in salted water.

Soup

- Before opening a tin of soup, shake well and open it at the bottom end instead of the top. The soup will slide out nicely.

Vegetables

- To restore a fresh flavour to frozen vegetables, pour boiling hot water over them, rinsing away all traces of the frozen water.
- Try cooking in broth for a nice flavour.

the
BEST
of hints for
THE
BATHROOM

Cleaning the bath

- For an extremely stained bath, use a mixture of peroxide and cream of tartar. Make a paste and scrub vigorously with a small brush. Rinse thoroughly.
- If stains persist, spread the above mixture over stains and apply a drop or two of household ammonia. Leave for two hours before scrubbing.
- Very old porcelain stains: Shave a bar of household soap into a bucket of hot water and add ½ cup of mineralised methylated spirit. Stir to dissolve the soap, then brush on stain vigorously.

More bath and sink cleaners

- Light stains can often be removed by simply rubbing with a cut lemon.
- For dark stains, and especially rust, rub with a paste of borax and lemon juice.
- To brighten up a bath which has yellowed, rub with a solution of salt and turpentine.

Clogged shower heads

- If your shower head is clogged, try boiling it in ½ cup vinegar and 1 quart water for 15 minutes.
- For plastic shower heads, soak in equal amounts of hot vinegar and water.

Ceramic tile

- Before you start cleaning the walls or tiles, run your shower a while with the hottest tap water available. Dirt loosened by steam will come off faster.
- For light jobs, wash with a solution of ½ cup ammonia,

41

$\frac{1}{2}$ cup white vinegar, $\frac{1}{4}$ cup washing soda and 1 gallon warm water.
- For extensive stains, make a paste of bicarbonate of soda and bleach, then scrub with a small brush. Rinse thoroughly.

Heavy shower stall film
- Rub lightly with a plain piece of dry steel wool (not the soap-filled variety). Try a patch first to be sure it isn't scratching your tile. If it is, you should use a finer piece of steel wool. As you scour the tile, you will see the scum coming right off. Wash down after the job is completed.

Washing shower curtains
- Fill the washing machine with warm water and add 2 large bath towels. Add $\frac{1}{2}$ cup each of detergent and bicarbonate of soda. Run through entire wash cycle. However, add 1 cup vinegar to the rinse water. Do not spin dry or wash vinegar out. This method will not work without the bath towels. Hang immediately. Wrinkles will disappear after curtain has thoroughly dried.

Removing mildew from shower curtains
- To prevent mildew, soak in a solution of salt water before hanging them for use.
- Use bicarbonate of soda to remove mildew from small areas.
- For stubborn stains on light coloured curtains, wash in above manner, followed by a rub-down with lemon juice.

Two excellent fixture cleaners
- To save time and money while providing the best shine possible to bathroom fixtures, use an old cloth

which has been dipped in paraffin. Paraffin removes scum quickly and the smell will only remain for a while.
- Spray fixtures liberally with a laundry soil-and-stain remover. Rub with cloth for an excellent shine.

Toilet rings
- Flush toilet to wet sides. Apply paste of borax and lemon juice. Leave for 2 hours and then scrub thoroughly.
- Or, rub with a fine grade of sandpaper. If the rings are years old, try wet-and-dry sandpaper (available at hardware shops).

Glass shower doors
- For a quick shine, rub with a sponge dampened in white vinegar.

What to do with your basic drip
- If the drip occurs during the night and you can't sleep, simply wrap a cloth around the opening of the tap.
- Or, tie a string to the tap, long enough to reach the drain. Water will run down the string noiselessly until you have time to fix it.

Sweet smells in the bathroom
- Add a touch of fragrance by dabbing your favourite perfume on a light bulb. When the light is on, the heat releases the aroma.

the
BEST
of hints for
BEAUTY

'Face it'
...these are going to be great hints

The greatest moisturiser
- Wash face thoroughly. While face is still wet rub in a tiny amount of petroleum jelly. Continue wetting face until the jelly is spread evenly and does not appear greasy. Many expensive health spas use this treatment, but they never reveal their secret. You will be surprised at how soft and smooth your face feels. Remember, it will not stay greasy if you keep adding water a little at a time.

Teach your skin not to be 'taut'
- Pour some apple cider vinegar into a basin of warm water and splash your face thoroughly. Allow to dry without using a towel. If used once a day, this will restore the natural ph-balance or acid mantle to your skin. Acne sufferers should try this also, but be sure to start with a perfectly clean face.
- Instead of splashing the solution on, spray it on your face. The spray bottle is always handy and you'll never forget.

Mineral water splash . . . fresher makeup

- After your face is thoroughly clean, spray with cold mineral water.
- After you have applied your makeup, spray your face with mineral water or soak tissue in mineral water and lightly dab it all over your face. Your makeup will stay fresh longer than usual.

The fastest way to dry up a blemish

- Dab it with lemon juice a few times a day.

The best deep pore cleanser around

- Bring a quart of water to the boil and take it to a table. Add the juice or peel of half a lemon and a handful of any herbs (rosemary, basil, thyme, mint . . .). Cover your hair with a shower cap and drape another towel over your head and the pot, holding your face about 12 inches above the water. With closed eyes, let your face steam for 15 minutes. Afterward, rinse with very cold water to close pores.
  Note: Do not use more than once a week or you will deplete your skin of too many natural oils.

A cheap but terrific facial scrub

- Make a paste of oatmeal and water. Apply to face and allow to dry until it feels tight. Rub off with your fingers, using lots of back and forth motion. This scrub sloughs off dead skin, gets rid of blackheads.

Sweeten your complexion with sugar

- Mix a teaspoon of sugar with soap lather and use the same as cleansing grains.

Treat yourself to a hot oil treatment

- For a professional hot oil treatment, saturate hair with olive, sesame or corn oil. Run the hottest water possible over 2 towels in your washing machine. After towels are wet, turn machine to spin cycle. Wrap head in plastic or aluminium foil before applying hot towels. Wait 20 minutes for best results. By using this method, your towels will be hot without the mess of dripping water.

Setting lotion

- A teaspoon of sugar or gelatin dissolved in a cup of warm water makes a handy setting lotion.
- Or, for an extra firm set, use your favourite flavour of jelly. That's right, fully prepared and ready to eat. Use as you would any jellied type of setting lotion.
- Also, try witch hazel or stale beer.

Hair conditioner

- Mayonnaise gives dry hair a good conditioning. Apply ½ cup mayonnaise to dry, unwashed hair. Cover with a plastic bag and wait for 15 minutes. Rinse a few times before shampooing thoroughly.

Final rinse

- For blondes, rinse hair with water containing a few tablespoons of lemon juice. For brunettes and red-heads, rinse with water containing several tablespoons of apple cider vinegar. Both will remove soapy film and give the hair a beautiful shine.
- Brunettes and redheads can also rinse their hair with coffee. Do not rinse it out. You will be amazed at how rich and shiny your hair will appear.

Homemade dry shampoo

- If regular shampooing is impossible, make your own

47

dry shampoo by mixing together 1 tablespoon salt and ½ cup maize flour or polenta. Transfer to a large-holed salt shaker, sprinkle it on oily hair lightly and brush out dirt and grime.

- Baby powder or cornflour can also be used as dry shampoos.

A quick hair set

- Instead of using electric rollers every day, try the following tip: Roll hair completely dry and cover with a warm damp towel for a few minutes. Allow hair to dry for a perfect quick set.

Terrific eye cream

- Before retiring, apply castor oil around your eyes. Make sure it is the odourless form. Plastic surgeons use it on their patients following surgery.

Manicure

- Mix 1 cup warm water and juice of ½ lemon. Soak fingertips 5 minutes. Rinse and pat dry, pushing back cuticles. Rub lemon peel against nail, back and forth vigorously. Finish by buffing with a soft cloth.

Quick drying nail polish

- For faster drying nail polish, put hands in a bowl of very cold water when nails are partially dry.
- Or, stick your hands in the freezer.

Non-stick nail polish bottle

- Treat a new bottle of nail polish by rubbing petroleum jelly inside the cover and on the grooves of the bottle. You will never have any trouble opening it, even after months.

You'll never have to throw away nail polish again

- Your nail polish will always be smooth and easy to apply if you store it in the refrigerator. Frosted nail polish will not separate either.
- However, if it has hardened or got to the gummy stage, place the bottle in a pan of boiling water. In no time the polish will be good as new.

Longer-lasting perfume

- Oily skin holds perfume scents longer than dry skin. So, before applying perfume, rub a very thin layer of Vaseline on your skin and you will smell delicious for hours.

Cucumber for tired eyes

- Place fresh cold cucumbers on your eyelids to rid them of redness and puffiness.

Make your own deodorant — two different ways

- Mix 2 tablespoons of alum into 1 pint warm water. Stir well. Add a small amount of your favourite cologne or after-shave lotion. Transfer to spray bottle.
- Or, mix 2 teaspoons of bicarbonate of soda, 2 teaspoons of petroleum jelly and 2 teaspoons of talcum powder. Heat in a double boiler over low heat and stir until smooth cream forms. Put cream in a small container with a tight lid and use as you would regular cream deodorant.

A 'berry' good treatment for teeth

- Dip a toothbrush in a mashed strawberry and brush vigorously to remove yellowing and stains.
- Or, brush with plain bicarbonate of soda until you see the difference.

Mending broken lipstick
- Heat the broken ends over a match until they melt enough to adhere when pressed together. Cool in refrigerator.

Sunburn relievers
- To cool down affected areas, rub with apple cider vinegar.
- Pat with a wet tea bag.
- Or, apply a paste of bicarbonate of soda and water.

the BEST of hints
for
THE CAR

Some hints
you 'auto' try

Washing your car

- Instead of washing your car with soap and water, try washing with a bucket of water and 1 cup paraffin, followed by a good wiping with soft cloths. The best part of it is that no matter how dirty your car is it will not need wetting down before starting, nor rinsing once you have finished. When it rains the car will actually bead off water. It helps prevent rust. Use no wax with this method.

Quick cleaning windows

- Bicarbonate of soda quickly cleans spatters and traffic grime from windscreen, headlights, chrome and enamel. Wipe with bicarbonate sprinkled on to a damp sponge. Rinse.
- Use plastic net bags (the kind onions come in) to wash windscreens when insects have accumulated. Simply tie a few bags into one bag and rub away.

Removing bumper stickers

- Use nail-polish remover or lighter fluid. Gently scrape away with a razor blade or knife.

Removing rust spots

- Briskly scrub the rust spots on your bumpers with a

piece of foil which has been crumpled, or use fine steel wool.
- Use a soap-filled steel wool pad.
- Paraffin helps too.

Scratches
- Take a matching colour crayon and work well into the scratch.

Tar remover
- Soak tar spots with raw linseed oil. Allow to stand until soft. Then, wipe with a soft cloth which has been dampened with the oil.
- Guess what? Peanut butter has also been known to remove tar.

To remove price tag sheets
- Sponge hot vinegar liberally on to the price sheets. Scrape gently. Continue applying vinegar until sheet is gone.
- Lemon extract works also.
- Or, apply salad oil. Leave for a while and scrape away.

Two parking hints
- On cold days and evenings, back your car into the garage. If needed, your car will be in good position for using jumper cables.
- If you have bumped the front bumper of your car into the back wall of your garage, try this: Suspend a small rubber ball on a string from the ceiling of the garage so that when the ball strikes your windscreen you will know the car is far enough in to close the garage door.

Ways to identify your car or bike
- Drop a business card or file card with your name and

address down the window slot. Just in case you have to prove the car is yours some day.

- To identify a stolen bicycle, even though the serial number may have been filed off, roll the file card around a pencil, remove the bicycle's seatpost and drop the card into the bicycle frame. It can easily be removed and shown as proof of ownership.

Cigarette ashes
- Ashes that continue to burn in the car ashtray are a nuisance. Prevent this by placing an inch of bicarbonate of soda (or gravel) in the bottom of the tray.

Battery corrosion—proofer
- Scrub battery terminals and holder with a strong solution of bicarbonate of soda and water. Then, smear with petroleum jelly.

Preventing doors and boot from freezing
- Wipe or spray the rubber gaskets with a heavy coating of vegetable oil. The oil will seal out water, but will not harm the gasket. This is especially good before having your car washed in the winter

Opening a frozen lock
- Heat the key with a cigarette lighter or match. Never force the key. Turn very gently.

Would you believe, a hair dryer will start your car?
- Before you call the car-starting service on cold mornings, remember this: your car will probably start if you blow hot air on the carburettor from a hair dryer. It works . . . it honestly does.

Salt remover for carpeting
- Combine equal amounts of vinegar and water to remove salt residue left behind from winter.

To eliminate windscreen freeze-up when parked outdoors
- Place your rubber floor mats over the windscreen. Secure the mat with windscreen wipers. You will save yourself the chore of scraping.

Make your own washer solvent that won't freeze
- Combine 1 quart surgical spirit, 1 cup water, 2 tablespoons liquid detergent. This formula is guaranteed not to freeze down to 35 degrees below zero.

Before you get stuck
- Place a bag of cat litter in your car boot, just in case you get stuck in the ice or snow. It provides excellent traction.

If you are stuck
- And there is no cat litter, sand or shovel available, remove the rubber mats from your car and place them in front of the rear wheels. You just might get out all by yourself.

the BEST
of hints for
THE CARPET

The first step is the most important!

- The first and most important step for preventing a spill turning into a stain is blotting up as much moisture as you possibly can. Scrape up any solids and blot with lots of clean towels. Begin at the outer edge of the stain and blot toward the centre. Do not rub because this will only spread the stain. And do not apply a spot remover until you have done a thorough job of blotting.

Stains be gone

- *For fresh stains:* Plain soda water is an instant spot remover and it is fantastic. Pour a little on the spot, let it stand for a few seconds and sponge up thoroughly.
- *For older stains:* Combine 2 tablespoons detergent, 3 tablespoons vinegar and 1 quart of warm water. Work into stain and blot as dry as possible.
- *Tide is the best stain remover for stubborn spots:* Make a sudsy solution of Tide laundry detergent and warm water. Brush the suds into the stain vertically and horizontally with a soft brush. Blot up excess. If the stain persists, repeat process. This works $9\frac{3}{4}$ times out of 10.

The last step is important too!

- After you've completed one of the above methods, cover the spot with a clean towel and place a heavy book on top of it. When the towel becomes damp replace it with a dry one.

An instant spot remover

- Try shaving cream. Foam is a good spot remover and it is ready instantly. Wash with water or soda water.

Repairing a burn

- Remove some fuzz from the carpet, either by shaving or pulling out with a tweezer. Roll into the shape of the burn. Apply a good cement glue to the backing of the rug and press the fuzz down into the burned spot. Cover with a piece of cleansing tissue and place a heavy book on top. This will cause the glue to dry very slowly and you will get the best results.

Flattened carpet

- If heavy furniture has flattened the pile of your rugs, raise it with a steam iron. Build up good steam and hold your iron over the damaged spot. Do not touch the carpet with the iron. Brush briskly.

Removing candle wax drippings

- Place blotting paper or brown paper over the spot and put a hot iron over the blotter. After a few minutes, the wax will be absorbed into the blotter. Repeat if necessary.

Repairing braided rugs

- Braided rugs often rip apart. Instead of sewing them use clear fabric glue to repair. It's that fast and easy.

57

Spot remover for indoor-outdoor carpeting
- Spray spots liberally with a pre-wash commercial spray. Leave it for several minutes, then hose down and watch the spots disappear.

A carpet brightener
- Sprinkle a generous amount of cornflour on your carpet. Leave for an hour before vacuuming. You will be amazed at the results.

Before you shampoo
- To prevent rust marks from forming on a wet carpet, put little plastic bags or small glass jars on each furniture leg. This also eliminates the dreadful job of moving furniture from one end of the room to the other.

Who tracked the mud in?
- Sprinkle cornflour on damp mud spots. Give it at least 15 minutes to soak up the mud, then vaccuum up and away.

Sooty footmarks
- Try an artgun eraser on light coloured carpets.
- Or, sprinkle soiled areas with salt. Wait $\frac{1}{2}$ hour and then vacuum.

Opposites attract
- Ever wanted to be a genius? Then, next time red wine spills on your carpet, remove it with white wine.

Removing chewing gum
- Press ice cubes against the gum until it becomes brittle and breaks off. Then use a spot remover to vanish last traces.

Glue

- Glue can be loosened by saturating the spot with a cloth soaked in vinegar.

Ballpoint ink marks

- Saturate the spot with hairspray. Allow to dry. Brush lightly with a solution of water and vinegar.

the
BEST
of
hints
for

CHILDREN

Tips for the newborn

- To allow mother a few extra hours' sleep, use the same perfume freely while at the hospital and when you get home. Later dab your perfume on baby's cot sheets or pillow. He will smell the mama smell and feel safe and content.
- If baby bubbles a bit after feeding and must have his vest changed frequently to keep him smelling sweet, try this: moisten a cloth with water, dip it in bicarbonate of soda and dab at the dribbled vest. The smell will disappear.
- Keep a heating pad (or hot water bottle) beside baby's cot and when he is up for his night feeds, turn the pad on warm and place on the cot mattress. When you put baby back down, his bed will be nice and warm and he will settle down more quickly. Be sure to remove the heating pad.

Make your own baby food

- Puree fresh vegetables, place in ice cube trays, and freeze for use at a later date.

Baby bottles

- Place a few agate marbles in the steriliser or a saucepan when cleaning bottles. The marbles will gather all the corrosion.
- Save a couple of empty soft-drink cartons and use them to hold baby bottles in the refrigerator. The bottles can be easily removed for access to anything stored behind.

A few hints for the sick or hurt child

- If your child has trouble swallowing a pill, place it in a teaspoon of applesauce and see how easily it goes down.
- An ice cream or lolly stick makes an excellent tongue depresser when checking for a sore throat.
- To remove a splinter from a child's finger, soak the injured part in any cooking oil for a few minutes. The splinter can be easily removed. Also, applying an ice cube to the finger for several minutes will numb the area and allow the splinter to be removed painlessly. Then you can kiss it and make it all better.
- To eliminate the 'ouch' when removing adhesive tape from your child's skin, just saturate a piece of cotton wool with baby oil and rub over the tape. It will come right off without hurting the skin.

Safety tips

- Even adults sometimes walk into closed, sliding glass doors. To help youngsters avoid this hazard, place a piece of coloured tape on the glass at eye level to alert the child when the door is closed.
- When your child reaches the crawling stage, tape the light flexes tightly around a table leg. This will prevent him from pulling lamps on to the floor. If you use transparent tape it will not mar the furniture.
- To protect your child from mashed fingers, place a cork at each end of the keyboard on the piano. Now, if the lid drops, his fingers are saved.
- If your toddler tries to sneak outside when you are not looking, try the old 'doorbell' trick. Tie a small bell to the door. You will always be able to hear when the door is being opened.

Baby's first pair of shoes

- For baby's first pair of hard-soled shoes, walking on a hard surface is like walking on ice for an adult. If you glue a very thin strip of foam rubber to the soles of the shoes, the baby will gain confidence when he is walking.

When foam rubber is worn, scrape off the remains with a razor blade and apply a new piece.

Teaching how to put shoes on
- To teach a child how to put the right shoe on the right foot, mark or tape the inside of the right shoe only.

Polishing baby shoes
- If the shoes are scuffed badly and do not seem to take the polish, rub them with a piece of raw potato or surgical spirit before polishing.
- After polishing, spray with hairspray to prevent polish from coming off so easily.
- Or, apply clear fingernail polish to the spots which scuff most frequently.

Tongue tied
- To prevent the tongues of your child's shoes from sliding out of place, cut two small, parallel slits in each tongue $\frac{1}{2}$ inch from the outside tip. After lacing, pull through the new slots and tie as usual.

A way to save disposable nappies
- If you ruin the adhesive tab on a nappy, simply tape the nappy with masking tape.

Dull nappy pins
- Simply stick the pins into a bar of soap.

Graduating from cot to bed
- Eliminate fears of injury when your child graduates from cot to full size bed by putting the cot mattress on the floor next to the bed. If the child falls out, he'll be startled but not hurt.

Bathing

- Use baby's infant seat for bathing in the full-size bath. Remove the pad and buckle strap and place a large folded bath towel on the seat and on the bath floor (to prevent slipping). Place baby in seat, and run water into bath. Now you can use both hands.
- When a child is past the baby bath stage, but is too small for the full-size bath, a plastic clothes basket with holes in it is ideal. Run several inches of water into the bath, place the basket in it and set your child in the basket.
- Put small pieces of soap into a white sock and tie up the open end. Children prefer it to a bar of soap and it will not slip from their hands.

When you are out of baby shampoo

- Shampoo will not run into eyes if you put petroleum jelly on baby's eyebrows and eyelids. The soap will run sideways instead of downward.
- Or, put a diving mask on your child. It's fun and he can watch the bubbles run down the mask without getting soap in his eyes. Peek-a-boo, I see you.

Calming the angry child

- Whispering works wonders when a child is angry. Simply whisper gentle words into his ear. He will stop crying so he can hear what you're saying. And 100% effective on husbands.

Saving your child's artwork and the appearance of your walls

- Give each drawing a good coating of hairspray and it will prevent the colour from fading or wearing off.

- To display his works of art, hang fishnet over one wall. Instead of ruining the wall by taping or tacking, simply pin his artwork to the fishnet with clothes pegs or pins.

5

Cleaning stuffed toys
- Clean with dry cornflour. Rub in, leave for a while, and brush off.

Soak up spills before they happen
- To eliminate messy spills when children are using paint or glue, cut an opening in the centre of a sponge and insert the container. The sponge keeps the container from tipping over, and absorbs any overflow.

Eliminating milk spills
- Your child will be able to hold on to a glass of milk better if you place two tight rubber bands around the glass an inch or so apart. This makes it easier for little hands to hold.

Lost and found
- Before leaving for a day at the zoo, fair or circus, tag each child with a stick-on label that gives his name, address and telephone number.

Keeping art supplies fresh
- Wrap new crayons with masking tape and there will be less chance of breaking.
- For fresh, smooth paste, moisten the lid with water before screwing the lid back on.

Ideas 'to boot'
- To avoid lost boots, cut two matching shapes of coloured tape and stick on the backs of each boot heel. Your child can easily spot them, even in a jumble of 30 pairs at school.

The growing jacket

- The life of a winter coat or jacket can be lengthened by sewing knitted cuffs (available in haberdashery departments) to the sleeves. Hopefully, your child might make it through another winter in last year's garment.

Removing gum from hair

- Rub ordinary cold cream into the hair. Pull down on the strands of hair several times with a dry towel.
- Or, rub in a dab of peanut butter. Massage the gum and peanut butter between your fingers until the gum is loosened. Remove with facial tissue.
- Freeze the hair with ice cubes and peel gum off hair.

Mirror, mirror on the wall

- To make your child's grooming chores less complicated, and out of respect for the little one, hang a second mirror at his eye level in the bathroom.

All dressed up and staying that way

- When you want to keep your children looking fresh for those special occasions, spray knees, cuffs and collars with fabric protector. The spills will bead up and wipe off easily to keep mum happy.

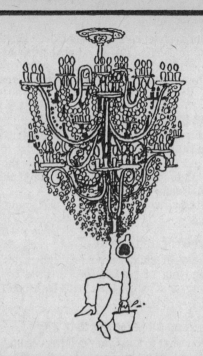

the BEST of hints for CLEANING THE MISCELL- ANEOUS

Artificial flowers
- Pour some salt into a large paper bag with the flowers. Shake vigorously. The salt won't look soiled at first, but wait until you see its colour when you run water on it.

Ball point pens
- If your ball point becomes clogged with excessive ink and fuzz, insert it in the filter portion of a cigarette. Just a few quick turns and it's ready for use.

Candles
- Sponge with a piece of cottonwool dampened with surgical spirit.
- Did you know? Candles burn more slowly and evenly with minimum wax drippings if you place them in the freezer for several hours before using.

Candle holders
- If your candle holders are coated with wax, place in the freezer for an hour or so. The wax will peel off in a jiffy with absolutely no injury to the silver.
- Or, run under very hot water and dry with a paper towel.

Canvas awnings
- Make old canvas look like new by painting with canvas paint (available at paint stores).
- Eliminate bird droppings with a stiff brush that has been run over a bar of household soap and sprinkled with dry washing soda. Hose well to rinse.

Cigarette smoke

- Soak a towel in water and swish it around the room. Smoke will disappear quickly.
- Put small bowls of vinegar in the corners of the room where smokers are congregating.
- Or, place activated charcoal in small dishes to remove post-party smells.
- Also, burn candles to eliminate the smoke.

Chandeliers

- Here is a method of cleaning crystal chandeliers which does not entail dismantling the fixture. The area underneath the chandelier should be protected by a plastic sheet. Fill a water tumbler with 1 part alcohol to 3 parts water. Raise the tumbler to each pendant until it is immersed. The crystal will drip-dry without leaving water spots, lint or finger marks. The crystal parts not accessible to the tumbler can be wiped with the solution.
- Or, wear cotton work gloves and dip your fingers in ammonia water and clean away.

Combs, brushes and curlers

- Add 3 tablespoons baking soda and 3 tablespoons household bleach to a basin of warm water. Swish around, rinse and drip-dry.

Curtains

- Before sending the curtains to the cleaners: As you remove the hooks, mark the places where the hooks were inserted with pink nail polish. These dots will remain through the cleaning process.
- For curtains that hang on particular windows, number the panels, starting from left to right. Use coloured thread and mark on the wrong side of the bottom hem. No. 1 panel, 1 long stitch; No. 2 panel, 2 long stitches,

etc. Be sure to knot the stitches well so that they will remain throughout the cleaning.

Diamonds

- Add some mild white soap flakes and a few drops of ammonia to a pot of boiling water. Place your diamond in a wire strainer and dip it into the boiling water for a few seconds. Let it cool, then rinse. Finally, soak it in a small bowl of alcohol for 10 minutes before drying on a piece of tissue paper.

Eyeglasses

- To clean eyeglasses without streaks, use a drop of vinegar or vodka on each lens.

Fireplaces

- There is less need to scrub the fireplace if you throw salt on the logs occasionally. This will reduce the soot by two-thirds.
- Vinegar will clean brick tiling around the fireplace. Dip a vegetable brush in white vinegar and scrub quickly. Immediately sponge to absorb the moisture.
- Rub smoked areas with an artgum eraser. This works especially well on porous, rock front fireplaces.
- For smooth stone or brick fireplaces, wash with a strong solution of sodium phosphate ($\frac{1}{2}$ cup to 1 gallon water). Apply with sponge. Use this solution only after all smoke possible has been erased by an artgum eraser.
- For big jobs: Add 4 ounces of household soap to 1 quart of hot water. Heat until soap dissolves. Cool, then stir in $\frac{1}{2}$ pound of powdered pumice and $\frac{1}{2}$ cup of household ammonia. Mix thoroughly. Remove as much of the smoky deposit as you can before applying a coat of the soap mixture with a paint brush. Allow it to remain on for 30 minutes. Scrub with a scrubbing

brush and warm water. Sponge with plenty of water to rinse.

Frames
- Wipe with a soft sponge moistened with turpentine. If the gilt seems a bit sticky after you finish, let dry for a day or two without touching.

Garage floors
- To remove oil drips from concrete: Soak with mineralised methylated spirit for 30 minutes and then scrub with a stiff brush as you add more mineralised methylated spirit. Immediately after the scrubbing, absorb the grease with oil towels or newspaper. Allow concrete to dry. Then, wash with a solution of laundry detergent, 1 cup bleach and 1 gallon of cold water. Repeat until stains are removed.
- Spread several thicknesses of newspaper over the area where quite a bit of oil has spilled. Saturate the newspaper with water and press firmly against the floor. Allow to dry thoroughly, remove, and the oil spots will be gone.
- To eliminate oil spots, sprinkle the area with sand or cat litter. They both will absorb the oil, and you can sweep it up.

Garden tools
- Quickly and easily remove rust by rubbing tools with a soap-filled steel wool pad dipped in paraffin or turpentine. Rub briskly with a piece of wadded aluminium foil.

Grills
- Barbecue grill: Tear off a sheet of heavy-duty aluminium foil large enough to completely cover your grill. Press foil shiny side down on grill and fold sides under,

covering as tightly as possible. When coals have nearly reached their hottest point, place grill over coals for ten minutes. Remove foil and any charred grease or food on your grill should drop off leaving your grill clean and shiny.

- Before ever using your barbecue grill, spray it heavily with vegetable oil.
- A fast and effective way to clean a grill is to use left-over brewed coffee. Pour it on a hot or cold grill. Wipe off and you will be amazed at the results.

Guitar
- Rub toothpaste on your guitar, let it dry, then buff for a super shine.

Household smells
- Here's a way to kill household smells and always have a fresh-smelling house for just pennies. Put a few drops of wintergreen oil (available at chemists) on a cotton-wool ball and place it in a glass container. It will last for months and is as effective as room sprays.
- Toss dried orange and lemon rinds into your fireplace for a spicy aroma.

Iron
- To remove mineral deposits from the inside of a steam iron, fill it with equal part of water and white vinegar. Let it steam for several minutes, then disconnect and leave for 1 hour. Empty, and rinse out with clear water.
- Remove brown or burned-on spots by rubbing with a heated solution of vinegar and salt.
- Remove wax build-up by rubbing with very fine sand-paper. Next, polish with a piece of fine soapless steel wool, then wipe off with a damp cloth.
- Or, clean the outside of your iron with toothpaste or silver polish.

Jewellery
- Clean with a soft cloth dabbed in toothpaste.

Pewter
- One of the best ways to clean pewter is to rub with cabbage leaves.
- Or, try a homemade mixture of wood ashes moistened with water.

Piano keys
- Apply toothpaste to a well dampened cloth. Rub the keys well, wipe dry and buff with a dry soft cloth.

Radiator
- Hang a damp cloth behind the radiator, then blow with the blower end of your vacuum cleaner. The dust and dirt will be blown into the damp cloth.

Telephone
- Clean your telephone with surgical spirit to keep it new looking.

Vases with small openings
- Dampen the inside of vase and add any toilet bowl cleaner. Leave to stand for 10 minutes and stains will disappear.

the BEST of hints for CLOTHING/ JEWELLERY/ SHOES

Longer lasting tights

- Before you ever wear a new pair of tights they should be frozen first. No kidding, they will last longer if you wet them thoroughly, ring out gently, place in a plastic bag and toss in the freezer. Once frozen, thaw in the bath and then hang to dry. It's a wild and crazy hint, but it's true!
- Or, starch them very, very lightly. This helps resist runs and they will also go on easily.

Stopping a ladder

- Apply hair spray or rub with a wet bar of soap. Of course, the old standby, clear nail polish, is still a good ladder stopper.

Before ever wearing a new garment

- Touch the centre of each button (front and back) with

clear nail polish. This will seal the threads and buttons will stay on much longer.

Clinging dresses
- Starch your slips to prevent dresses from clinging.
- Run a wire coat hanger between your dress and nylon slip. This will draw out the electricity and eliminate some of the clinging.

A wrinkle-free idea
- Hang your wrinkled garment on the curtain rail in your bathroom and run the hottest water possible from your bath or shower. Close the bathroom door and let the water run for a while. This allows the steam to penetrate the material, thus eliminating the wrinkles. When travelling this hint should be remembered.

A great cover-up
- If you are in a hurry and notice a stain on your white suit, cover it up by rubbing baby powder into the stain.

Shave away fuzz balls
- Remove those little balls of fuzz from an old shirt collar by going over the surface with a clean shaver. It will not harm the fabric.

The above trick works on sweaters too!
- Remove knots and balls from sweater by shaving with a regular razor (very gently) or an electric shaver.
- Or, remove by rubbing with a very fine piece of sandpaper.

Sticky zippers
- They will slide easily if rubbed with a lead pencil.

Removing hem creases

- White vinegar will help remove a permanent crease. Sponge the material liberally with the vinegar and press with a warm iron.
- Try this trick when lengthening old jeans: The white hem lines will disappear if you mix permanent blue ink with a little water (keep adding water until you get the perfect shade). Then, apply with a small brush. Let dry and no more telltale hemline.

A quick pair of ski jeans

- Convert regular jeans into ski pants by spraying with a waterproof fabric protector.

In case you need it . . . here's another jean trick

- Many times the cuffs on jeans will turn up after they have been washed. To correct this, affix a wide strip of iron-on mending material (the kind used for patching) to the inside of the cuffs. You will have no more problems with cuffs turning up.

Simple jewellery re-stringing

- Use the finest fishing line to re-string a broken necklace. The line is firm enough so that you do not need a needle, but soft enough to hand string beautifully.
- When re-stringing beads of graduated sizes, tape down a strip of cellophane tape (sticky side up) on a smooth surface. Arrange beads in order before re-stringing.

Eliminating a knot

- If a necklace chain is knotted, put a drop or two of salad oil on a piece of waxed paper, lay the knot in the oil and undo it by using 2 straight pins. It should unknot easily.

These 'shoe' be great hints ...
and more to 'boot'

Polishing and cleaning

- Nail-polish remover is excellent for removing tar and grease from white shoes. Do not use on plastic.
- Use a solution of equal amounts of vinegar and water to remove salt stains from shoes and boots.
- Give your patent leather shoes a bright shine by rubbing with a dab of petroleum jelly.
- Use household window spray or furniture polish as a speedy shoe shine for all types of leather.
- Your white shoe polish will go on evenly if you rub the shoes with surgical spirit or a raw potato before applying the polish.
- White shoe polish will not smear if you spray the shoe with hair spray after it has dried thoroughly.

Drying tips

- A sure way to dry children's boots fast: Drop the hose of a portable hair dryer into the boot. Let it run until the boot is completely dry.
- To dry a pair of shoes quickly, hang them under a chair by hooking the heels on the chair rungs. They will be out of the way and still receive circulation of air on both sides.
- Keep rain-soaked shoes from becoming stiff by rubbing well with saddle soap before they have dried. Dry

away from direct heat. When thoroughly dry give them a good polishing.

Some hints you should know about canvas shoes

- Spray new canvas or rope-trimmed shoes with a fabric protector to keep them looking new.
- To clean rope-trimmed canvas shoes, rub with a toothbrush that has been dipped in rug shampoo.
- Keep new white tennis shoes looking new by spraying heavily with starch.

the BEST of hints for

THE FLOOR

Hints
that will 'floor' you

A good cleaning agent
- For varnished floors or woodwork of any kind, rub with cold tea.

Eliminating marred floors
- When moving furniture slip old heavy socks over their legs.

A fast cover-up
- Renovate floors which have become faded in spots by mixing brown shoe polish with floor wax and applying to spots. It will give the floor an antique look.

Silence squeaks forever
- Silence floor squeaks by dusting talcum powder or dripping glue into the cracks.

Rub those scratches away
- With a piece of very fine steel wool dipped in floor wax.

Removing heel marks
- Wipe the spots with paraffin or turpentine.
- Or, try an ordinary pencil eraser.

Removing tar spots
- Use paste wax. This also works on shoes.

Nail polish spills
- To remove nail polish from waxed floors or tile, let it solidify before attempting removal. When the polish is barely solid and pliable it can be peeled off. Smears are removed by wiping up the polish before it has dried, or by using a solvent on completely hardened polish.

Removing crayon marks
- Remove from vinyl tile or linoleum with silver polish.

A quick shine between waxings
- Mop with a piece of waxed paper under your mop. The dirt will also stick to the waxed paper.

Nylon stockings for dusting
- Place a nylon stocking over your floor mop. Discard the stocking and you will have a clean mop.

Loose linoleum edges easy to fix
- Work linoleum cement (available at hardware shops) under the loosened edge of the corner, using a blunt knife. Put a few heavy books over the area and let dry for 24 hours.

To seal linoleum seams
- Run a strip of cellophane tape down the full length of the cracks. Paint clear varnish over the tape and the surface will hold up indefinitely.

A faster working carpet sweeper

- Dampen the brushes of your carpet sweeper before using and it will do a much better job of picking up lint and string.

Cleaning your floor polisher

- If wax has built up on the felt pads of your floor polisher, place the pads between several thicknesses of paper towelling and press with a warm iron. The towels will quickly absorb the old wax.

the BEST
of hints for
FURNITURE

Fantastic furniture polish

- Use $\frac{1}{3}$ cup each boiled linseed oil, turpentine and vinegar. Mix together and shake well. Apply with a soft cloth and wipe completely dry. Wipe again with another soft cloth. Do not try to boil your own linseed oil – it is not the same. Buy it at a hardware or paint shop.
- Or, add a teaspoon of apple cider vinegar to your favourite liquid furniture polish.

To remove polish build-up

- Mix $\frac{1}{2}$ cup vinegar and $\frac{1}{2}$ cup water. Rub with a soft cloth that has been moistened with solution, but wrung out. Dry immediately with another soft cloth.

Polishing carved furniture

- Dip an old soft toothbrush into furniture polish and brush lightly.

Is your seat sagging?

- Tighten a drooping cane chair seat by giving it a hot water bath and placing it outside in the sunlight to dry and shrink. After it has dried thoroughly, apply either lemon or cedar oil to prevent cracking and splitting.
- Sagging springs in chair: Turn the chair upside down. Make a pattern of the upper-structure frame. Transfer the pattern either to a piece of scrap masonite or plywood ($\frac{1}{8}$ inch). Nail to the upper structure. By doing this, the springs are pushed back into the chair, eliminating the sag.

Cigarette burns

- Burns can be disguised by touching up the bare spot with matching coloured varnish. Paint on several coats of the varnish until the surface is level. But always consider the value of the furniture. It might be better to have a professional make the repair.
- Or, make a paste of bath-brick and salad oil. Rub into the burned spot only, following the grain of the wood. Wipe clean with a cloth that has been dampened in oil. Wipe dry and apply your favourite furniture polish.

Removing paper that is stuck to a wood surface

- Do not scrape with a knife. Pour any salad oil, a few drops at a time, on the paper. Leave for a while and rub with a soft cloth. Repeat the procedure until the paper is completely gone.
- Old transfers can be removed easily by painting them with several coats of white vinegar. Give the vinegar time to soak in, then gently scrape off.

Scratches

- *Make sure you always rub with the grain of the wood when repairing a scratch.*
- *Walnut:* Remove the meat from a fresh, unsalted walnut. Break it in half and rub the scratch with the broken side of the nut.
- *Mahogany:* You can either rub the scratch with a dark brown crayon or buff with brown paste wax.
- *Red Mahogany:* Apply ordinary iodine with a number 0 artist's brush.
- *Maple:* Combine equal amounts of iodine and white spirit. Apply with a Q-tip, then dry, wax and polish.

- *Ebony:* Use black shoe polish, black eyebrow pencil or black crayon.
- *Teakwood:* Rub very gently with 0000 steel wool. Rub in equal amounts of linseed oil and turpentine.
- *Light finished furniture:* Scratches can be hidden by using tan shoe polish. However, use only on shiny finishes.
- *For all minor scratches:* Cover each scratch with a generous amount of white petroleum jelly. Allow it to remain on for 24 hours. Rub into wood. Remove excess and polish as usual.
- *For larger scratches:* Fill with plastic wood and touch up with matching varnish.

Two solutions to remove white water rings and spots

- Dampen a soft cloth with water and put a dab of tooth-paste on it. For stubborn stains, add bicarbonate of soda to the toothpaste.
- Make a paste of butter or mayonnaise, and cigarette ashes. Apply to spot and buff away with a slightly damp cloth. Polish as usual.

Marble table-top stains

- Sprinkle salt on a freshly cut lemon. Rub very lightly over stain. Do not rub hard or you will ruin the polished surface. Wash off with soap and water.
- Scour with a water and bicarbonate of soda paste. Let stand for a few minutes before rinsing with warm water.
- For horrible marble stains, try this: Place the marble table in hot sunlight. If this is not possible, heat the marble for 1 hour or more under a hot spotlight (never a sun-lamp). Then, swab on white household bleach. Continue this every hour or so until discolouration is gone. (Sometimes this may take a couple of days). Rinse with water and dry. Move to shade and polish

with hard wax. Never use oil polish or soft waxes on marble; they can cause discolouration.

Removing candle wax from wooden finishes
- Soften the wax with a hair dryer. Remove wax with paper towelling and wash down with a solution of vinegar and water.

Proper cleaning and care for leather table tops
- Remove all wax build-up with a vinegar and water solution ($\frac{1}{4}$ cup vinegar and $\frac{1}{2}$ cup water). To raise any indentations such as pressure points from lamps or ash trays, apply lemon oil to the leather twice a day for a week. To maintain results, use lemon oil monthly.

Plastic table tops
- You will find that a coat of Turtle Wax is a quick pick-up for dulled plastic table tops and counters.
- Or, rub in toothpaste, and buff.

Glass table tops
- Rub in a little lemon juice. Dry with paper towels and shine with newspaper for a sparkling table.
- Toothpaste will remove small scratches from glass.

Chrome cleaning
- For sparkling clean chrome without streaks, use a cloth dampened in ammonia.

Removing glue from furniture
- Aeroplane or cement glue can be removed by rubbing with cold cream, peanut butter or salad oil.

Tips for wicker
- To keep wicker furniture from turning yellow, wash with a solution of warm salt water.
- To prevent drying out, apply lemon oil once in a while.
- Never let wicker freeze. This will cause cracking and splitting.
- Wicker needs moisture, so use a humidifier in the winter.

Removing rust on metal furniture
- A good scrubbing with turpentine should accomplish the job.

Proper cleaning and care of vinyl upholstery
- Never oil vinyls because oil will make the vinyl hard. If this happens it is almost impossible to soften it again. For proper cleaning, sprinkle bicarbonate of soda or vinegar on a rough damp cloth. Then, wash with a very mild dishwashing soap. Body oil will cause vinyl to become hard so it should be cleaned once in a while.

Leather upholstery
- Clean with a damp cloth and saddle soap.
- Prevent leather from cracking by polishing regularly with a cream made of 1 part vinegar and 2 parts linseed oil.

Removing blood stains from upholstery
- Cover the spot immediately with a paste of cornflour and cold water. Rub lightly and place object in the sun to dry. The sun will draw the blood out into the cornflour. Brush off. If the stain is not completely gone, try, try again.

Grease and oil stains
- Sprinkle talcum, cornflour, or Fullers Earth on a fresh stain. Rub in well and let stand until the stain is absorbed. Brush off and wipe with a damp cloth.

Soiled cotton upholstery
- Try rubbing the soiled areas with artgum squares. Purchase at any stationery shop.

Ready-to-use upholstery cleaner
- Shaving cream is one of the most useful upholstery cleaners for new stains and ordinary dirt.
- Make your own by mixing $\frac{1}{2}$ cup mild detergent with 2 cups boiling water. Cool until it forms into jelly, then whip with a hand beater for good stiff foam.

the **BEST**
of hints for

THE HANDY PERSON

Wobbly chair legs

- Secure a loose chair leg by wrapping the loose end with a small strip of nylon hose or thread before applying the glue, then re-insert.
- A few drops of wood expander will achieve the same results.

Wobbly table

- If your table wobbles because of a short leg, put a small amount of Plastic Wood on waxed paper. Set the short leg on it and allow to dry. Trim down with a sharp knife and smooth with sandpaper.

Sticky dresser drawers

- They will slide easily again if you rub candle wax or soap on the runner of the side that seems to be sticking.

Is your screw loose?

- Stick a wooden kitchen match in the screw hole and break it off. Then, put the screw back in.
- Wind a few strands of steel wool around the threads of the screw before screwing it in.
- Paint the screw of a wobbly drawer knob with fingernail polish before inserting it. When the polish dries, it will hold the screw tightly.
- Or, dip in glue or putty and it will hold tight.

Difficulty loosening a tight screw

- Heat the edge of a screwdriver to its hottest point before loosening a screw.

- Or, put a few drops of peroxide on the tight screw and soak for a few minutes.

Remember this
- Left is loose and right is tight.

Loosening a rusted bolt
- You can often loosen a rusted bolt by applying a cloth soaked in any carbonated beverage.
- A drop or two of ammonia will loosen it right up.
- Before screwing it back in, wrap thread around it and coat with Vaseline to avoid future rusting.

Not just another screwy idea
- Should metal screws on your home appliance keep coming loose, a dab of *shellac* placed under the heads before tightening them, holds them securely in place.

To loosen joints
- Put vinegar in a small oil can and apply liberally to joints to loosen old glue.

Longer lasting sandpaper and easier sanding
- Sandpaper will last longer, work better and resist cracking if the paper backing is dampened slightly, then wrapped around a block of wood.

Mending a leaking vase
- Coat the inside with a thick layer of paraffin wax and allow it to harden. The paraffin wax will last indefinitely and the vase will not leak.

Cutting plywood
- Prevent plywood from splitting by putting a strip of

masking tape at the point where you plan to start sawing.

How to find a wall stud
- Hold a pocket compass level with the floor and at a right angle to the wall. Slowly move it along the surface of the wall. Movement of the compass needle will indicate the presence of nails and reveal the stud location. Wall studs are usually 16 inches apart, centre to centre.

Preventing nylon cord and rope from fraying
- Dip the ends of the rope in varnish and it will not unravel.
- To prevent nylon cord or twine from fraying at a cut end, heat the end over a small flame. The strands will bond into a solid unit. Knots can be prevented from working loose by this same method.

Preventing rust on tools
- Place a piece of charcoal, chalk or several mothballs in your toolbox to attract any moisture.
- Wax tools with a car paste wax. A light coat will ward off corrosion for quite some time.
- Or, store small tools in a bucket of sand.

Preventing a screwdriver from slipping
- Rub chalk on the blade.

Stop squeaks
- Use nonstick vegetable spray to lubricate squeaky hinges, sticky locks, bicycle chains, roller skate wheels and so on.

After sanding a surface
- Pull on old nylon stocking over your hand and rub

lightly over the wood. You will be able to locate the slightest rough spot.

Finding a gas leak

- Lather the pipes with soapy water. The escaping gas will cause the soapy water to bubble, revealing the damaged areas. You can make a temporary plug by moistening a cake of soap and pressing it over the spot. When the soap hardens it will effectively close the leak until the gasman comes.

More hints for the handy person

- For accuracy in drilling metal, use a small drill first.
- When drilling hard metal, add a drop or two of turpentine to the drill point instead of oil for lubrication.
- A small quantity of paraffin will help ease a hand saw through a tight cut.
- Thaw a frozen water pipe with a hair dryer.
- To prevent snow from sticking to a shovel, cover shovel with spray wax.

Picture perfect

For cockeyed pictures try this:
- Wind some adhesive tape around the centre of the picture wire. The wire will be less likely to slip on the hanger.
- Place masking tape on the back four corners of your picture and press against the wall.
- Or, wrap masking tape (sticky side out) around the middle of a rounded toothpick and place a few near the bottom, back side of the frame.

Preventing experimental holes when hanging pictures
- Cut a paper pattern of each picture or mirror that you plan to hang and pin to the wall. After you've found the correct positions for the hangers, perforate the paper with a sharp pencil to mark the wall.
- Before you drive nails into the wall, mark the spot with an X of cellophane tape. This trick will keep the plaster from cracking when you start hammering.
- A wet fingerprint shows the exact spot for the hanger. The print dries without a mark.

Finishing unfinished picture frames

- Stain them beautifully with ordinary liquid shoe polish. Apply one coat and let it dry. Follow with another coating. Then, wax with a good paste wax. Brown polish gives the wood a walnut glow and oxblood polish emulates a rich mahogany. Tan polish will appear as a light maple colour.

the BEST of hints for
THE
LAUNDRY

Did you know?

- The basic ingredient of many commercial spot removers is 2 parts water to 1 part surgical spirit.

Cleaning your machine

- Fill the washer with warm water and pour a gallon of distilled vinegar into it. Run the machine through an entire cycle. The vinegar will cleanse the hoses and unclog soap scum from them.

Ring around the collar

- Use a small paint brush and brush hair shampoo into soiled shirt collars before laundering. Shampoo is made to dissolve body oils.
- Mark heavily with chalk. The chalk will absorb the oils and once the oil is removed. the dirt will come off easily. This method may require a few applications if the yellow line has been there for some time. If the shirt is new, one application should do it.
- Or, apply a paste of vinegar and bicarbonate of soda. Rub in and wash as usual. This method also removes dirt and mildew.

No more fluff

- To remove fluff from corduroy, wash and allow to dry very slowly. While clothing is still damp, brush with a clothes brush. All the fluff will come off, but remember, the clothing must be damp.
- You will eliminate the fluff problem by adding 1 cup white vinegar to the final rinse cycle.

- Or, put a yard of nylon netting into the dryer with wet clothes to act as a fluff catcher.
- If the fluff, under and around the filter of dryer seems damp, it means the outside vent is clogged. You'd better clean it out before the machine breaks down.

The final rinse cycle

- To make sure clothes receive a thorough rinsing, add 1 cup white vinegar to the rinse cycle. This will help dissolve the alkalines in soaps and detergents. Plus, it will give you soft and sweet-smelling clothing for just pennies.
- The vinegar is a must for hand washing. It cuts down soap so fast you will only have to rinse twice.
- A teaspoon of Epsom salts to a gallon of rinse water will help keep most materials from fading or running.

Creme rinse your sweater

- For the best results when hand washing sweaters, put a capful of creme hair rinse in the final rinse water.
- Or, rinse wool garments in lukewarm water and a few tablespoons of glycerine. This will keep them soft and will also help prevent itching when they are worn.

Accidentally washed woollen item

- Soak in tepid water to which you have added a good hair shampoo. Sometimes this will soften the wool fibres enough to allow for a reshaping. It's worth a try.

Washing feather pillows

- First check for any open or weak seams. Place the pillow in a pillowcase. Wash 2 pillows at a time for a balanced load or add towels for balance. Fill your washer with warm water and push pillows down to saturate them completely before turning on the gentle cycle. Stop the washer halfway through the washing and turn pillows over. To dry, put feather pillows (not foam rubber) into dryer along with a *clean tennis shoe.* Drying will take up to 2 hours.

Renovating feather pillows

- Set dryer on air setting and let pillows tumble for 15 minutes. However, make sure there are no holes in the pillows or the feathers will work through.

Machine washing dainty garments

- Drop your dainty garments into a pillowcase and fasten the loose end with a plastic bag tie. Place in washer and wash on a gentle cycle.

Too many suds

- Any time your washing machine overflows from too many suds, pour in a little fabric softener. Suds will disappear.

Procedure for cleaning velvet

- To clean, raise nap and remove wrinkles. Hold garment (pile side up) over steaming water to which a little ammonia has been added. Finish by brushing well and ironing lightly on the wrong side.

Renovating stiffened chamois
- Soak in warm water to which a spoonful or so of olive oil has been added.

When the red wine spills
- Sprinkle the spill immediately with lots of salt. Dunk into cold water and rub the stain out before washing.

Cleanest work clothes ever
- Add ½ cup of household ammonia to the wash water.

Removing grease from suede
- Sponge with a cloth dipped in vinegar or soda water. Restore nap of suede by brushing with a suede brush.

Getting white cotton socks white again
- Boil in water to which a slice of lemon has been added.

A fast way to dampen clothes
- Place clothes in dryer and add 2 thoroughly wet bath towels. Set dryer on a no-heat setting and let clothing tumble until desired dampness.
- If you have dampened ironing that you can't finish, stick it in the freezer until you are ready to catch up.

Faster ironing
- Place a strip of heavy duty aluminium foil over the entire length of the ironing board and cover with pad. As you iron, heat will reflect through to the underside of the garment.
- Starch your ironing board cover. This also helps the cover stay clean longer.

Ironing embroidery
- Lay the embroidery piece upside down on a turkish towel before ironing. All the little spaces between the embroidery will be smooth when you are finished.

Removing alcoholic beverage stains
- Soak fresh stains in cold water and a few tablespoons of glycerine (*available at chemists*). Rinse with white vinegar and water. These stains turn brown with age so treat immediately.

Blood
- Cover area with meat tenderiser. Apply cool water to make a paste. Wait 15–30 minutes, sponge with cool water.

Chewing gum
- Place garment in plastic bag and put in freezer. Scrape off frozen gum.
- Or, loosen gum by soaking in white vinegar or rubbing with egg white before laundering.

Candle wax or wax crayon
- Place the stained area between clean paper towels or pieces of brown paper and press with a warm iron.

Grease on double knit
- Soda water works wonders for removing grease from double-knit fabrics.

Fruit stains
- Remove stain by stretching the stained area over a bowl and pouring boiling water, from a height of several feet, through the stain.

Ballpoint ink

- Apply hairspray liberally to stain. Rub with a clean dry cloth and the ink usually disappears. This works exceptionally well on polyester fabrics.
- Or, try rubbing alcohol on the spot before laundering.

Iron mould

- Apply lemon juice and salt, then place in the sun.
- Rust can also be removed from white washables by covering the stains with cream of tartar, then gathering up the ends of the article so that the powder stays on the spot. Dip the entire spot into hot water for about 5 minutes. Ordinary laundering will complete the job.

Mildew

- Dry in the sun after moistening with lemon juice and salt.
- On leather, sponge with equal amounts of water and surgical spirit.

Perspiration

- Soak the garment in warm vinegar water.

Scorch

- On whites, sponge with a piece of cotton which has been soaked in peroxide. Use the 3 per cent solution sold as a mild antiseptic.
- For linen and cotton, dampen a cloth with peroxide, lay it on the scorched area and iron with a warm iron.

Shoe polish

- Remove with surgical spirit. Use 1 part spirit and 2 parts water on coloured fabric. Use it straight on whites.

Tar

- Rub the tar spot with paraffin until removed, then wash with detergent and water. The paraffin will not take the colour out of most fabrics, but you'd better test it first.

the BEST
of hints for
THE
PAINTER

Painting windows

- To eliminate window scraping try these tips: Dampen strips of newspaper or any other straight-edged paper with warm water. Spread strips around each window pane, making sure that the paper fits tightly into corners and edges. The paper will cling until you have finished with the paint job.
- Rub a bar of softened soap around the window panes.
- Or, swab on liquid detergent with a paint brush (a few inches from the frame). When the window's dry, paint away.
- Before painting windows, remove the hard-to-get dirt out of nooks and crannies with an old paint brush.

Spattered paint on windows and woodwork

- If the paint spatters on windows use nail-polish remover. Allow to soak for a few minutes then rub off with a cloth and wash with warm suds. The paint will usually disappear, no matter how long it has been there.
- Soften old stains with turpentine and scrape off with a razor blade. This method also works on putty stains.
- Wash freshly dried paint off glass with a hot vinegar solution.
- Apply a coat of lemon oil on woodwork before painting walls. If paint speckles appear they will rub off easily.
- Coat door hinges, doorknobs, lock latches and other hardware with a coating of petroleum jelly. This will eliminate a lot of scraping after.

Drip catchers

- When painting the ceiling, you can prevent drops from

landing on your head by simply sticking the paint brush through the middle of a paper plate and securing with Scotch tape.

- Before painting a chair or table, place jar lids under each leg to catch paint drips.
- To prevent drips of paint from falling on your light fixtures, tie plastic bags around them.

Storing leftover paint

- To prevent scum forming on leftover paint, place a disc of aluminium foil directly on the paint surface. To make the disc the correct size, set the can on the foil and cut around it.
- Keep oil-base paint fresh by adding 4 tablespoons of mineralised methylated spirit only to the top layer of the paint. Do not mix until the next paint job.
- Tightly fit the lids of paint containers and store upside down. Scum will not form on paint.
- Always mark the paint level and colour on each can before storing.
- Use nail-polish or shoe-polish bottles for leftover paint and label. They are excellent for small touch-ups.
- When tiny touch-ups are necessary, use throw-away Q-tips instead of soiling a dry paint brush.

Cleaning paint brushes

- A new paint brush will last longer and be much easier to clean if it soaks in a can of linseed oil for 12 hours before it is ever used.
- To soften hard paint on brushes, soak in hot vinegar. Follow with a wash in warm, sudsy water.
- After washing brushes and rollers, use a fabric softener in the final rinse water. It helps them stay soft and pliable.
- Use a lidded tin when cleaning paint brushes with paint thinner. After the brushes have been cleaned, cover the tin and let stand for a few days. The paint will settle to

the bottom and you can pour the clean thinner into another tin and re-use.

Fast clean-ups

- When working on a paint job which takes a couple of days, save time by thoroughly wrapping brushes in several layers of foil and freezing (stick them right into the freezer compartment of your refrigerator). Let brushes defrost an hour or more before returning to the job.
- Put a large plastic bag over your roller pan before putting the paint in. When you have finished, throw the bag away.

Banishing paint smells

- Add 2 teaspoons of vanilla extract per quart of paint.
- Place a large dish of water which contains a tablespoon of ammonia in the freshly painted room. Leave overnight.
- Or, place a large cut onion into a big pan of cold water. Paint smells will sponge into the onion within a very short time.

Lumpy paint

- The best strainer of all is an old nylon stocking.
- An old egg beater is excellent for stirring paint.
- Cut a circle of fine wire mesh slightly smaller than the can lid. As the mesh settles, it will carry all lumps to the bottom.

Stick it!

- After painting, apply some of the paint to an ice cream or lolly stick. It is a handy colour guide to matching colours when shopping.

Preventing white paint from yellowing
- Stir a drop of black paint into any good white paint.

Paint removers for face and hands
- Cooking oil or baby oil is a better way to remove paint because it will not burn the skin.
- For easy removal, rub Vaseline on exposed skin.
- Before painting, give fingernails a good coating of bar soap for the fastest wash ever.

Before puttying windows
- Mix putty with the paint that matches the woodwork.

Antiquing furniture
- Try using a small piece of carpet to work in the glaze. It gives a beautifully grained effect.

the BEST of hints for
PETS/PESTS

What to do about those doggy spots
- Blot up as much moisture as possible. Rub with a solution of vinegar or lemon juice and warm sudsy water. Blot and blot some more. Then pour undiluted soda water over the spot. Blot again. Place a dry towel over the stain and put a heavy book on top of it. If the towel becomes soggy, immediately replace with a clean, dry one.

What if the cat makes a mistake
- Follow the above procedure, but once the spot has dried, rub with a cloth dampened in ammonia. This will not only take away the offensive smell, but it will prevent the cat from ever doing it again in the same spot.

More rub-a-dub-dub hints
- A creme rinse is helpful for dogs whose fur tangles when wet.
- To cut soap film and wash away strong soap smells, add vinegar or lemon juice to the rinse water.
- For whiter and brighter fur, put a little blueing in the shampoo or rinse water.
- If your pet is moulting, place a tea strainer in the drain to keep pipes from clogging up.

Removing burrs
- Remove burrs by working oil into the tangle or by crushing the burrs with pliers. Crushed burrs lose their holding power and can be combed out.

Dry cleaning your dog
- Instead of always giving your dog a bath, rub bicarbonate of soda into his coat thoroughly and then brush off. It deodorises as well as it cleans.

Giving your dog a pill
- Most dogs love chocolate, so if yours refuses to swallow a pill, push the tablet into a piece of softened chocolate. You could also hide the pill in a chunk of dog food.

Chewing puppy
- If your new pup is chewing on your table and chair legs, solve the problem by dabbing a little oil of cloves (available at chemists) on the wood with a piece of cotton. If the smell does not keep him away, the bitter taste will.
- Help prevent damage to rugs and shoes by giving him a thoroughly washed out plastic bleach bottle to chew on.

Whining puppy

- Your puppy probably misses his mother. So make him feel at home by putting a warm hot water bottle, wrapped in a towel, and a ticking clock in his bed. Sometimes a radio playing soft music will help also.

Keeping the cat off your favourite chair

- Stuff a few mothballs in the cushion of a chair or sofa and your cat will stay clear.
- Cats hate plastic coverings! Cover your chair until your cat realises the chair is a no-no.

Fleas will 'flee'

- If you place some fresh pine needles in his kennel or underneath his bedding.
- Or, salt the crevices of his kennel and wash him periodically with salt water.

A safety tip for 'Rover'

- Tape reflector tape on your dog's or cat's collar to help cut down the danger of its being struck by a car at night.

Keeping the flies and stray dogs away from the garbage

- To prevent flies from swarming around rubbish bins, hose them down and allow to dry in the sun. Then, sprinkle a little dry soap into them.
- If you are hounded by stray dogs attacking the garbage, sprinkle full strength ammonia over the garbage bags before placing them in the bin.

Silverfish

- Sprinkle a mixture of boric acid and sugar on affected areas.

There's a bee in the house

- If a wasp or bee gets into the house, reach for the hairspray. Most insect sprays only infuriate them, but the hairspray stiffens their wings, immobilising them immediately. This works on all winged insects.

How to treat bug bites

- Treat insect bites with a poultice of either cornflour or bicarbonate of soda, mixed with vinegar, fresh lemon juice or witch hazel.
- Apply a paste made of meat tenderiser and water.
- Or, rub bites with wet bar soap to help relieve itching.

Bee stings

- Apply a poultice of bicarbonate of soda and water.
- Or, try applying a fresh cut slice of raw onion to the sting to help draw out the poison. Hold the onion in place with adhesive tape.

the BEST of hints for
PLANTS/
FLOWERS/
GARDENS

Watering houseplants

- Use water at room temperature. A plant can be injured by cold water.
- Let tap water stand for 1 day to rid water of chlorine. This will help avoid brown tips.
- Stick your finger 1 inch into top soil, if it feels moist, delay watering.
- The water you boil eggs in is filled with minerals and is a good drink for your plants.
- Or, drop egg shells into a jar of water and cover. Leave to stand a day before watering. Do not store egg shells for any length of time, because they will spoil and cause the worst smell.
- Top choice fertilisers are old aquarium water and water in which fish has been frozen.
- Don't throw away your fizzless soda water. It has just the right chemicals to add vigour and colour to your plants.
- Once in a while, if you wish to water plants in hanging baskets without making a mess, try using ice cubes. They will not drip through before being absorbed. But only once in a while.
- Bulb plants should always be watered from the bottom. Fill a saucer or kitchen sink with water and let the plant sit in it.
- If you have a room full of plants, a small portable vaporiser is a must for addition of moisture in the wintertime.

Snow your plants with kindness

- Scoop up some clean snow and let it melt. Use it for watering because there are wonderful minerals in snow.

'Love 'em and leave 'em'

- To water houseplants while on holiday, stand plants on bricks submerged in water in the bath. The bricks absorb water, keeping the plants happy.
- Or, place all houseplants in the bath on old thickly folded bath towels, in a few inches of water. They will absorb moisture as needed.
- You might want to try this hint: Place one end of a clothesline into a pail of water and bury the other end in the plant soil. Make sure the water pail is higher than the plant.

To keep indoor plants growing straight

- Frequently rotate the pots about a quarter of a turn so they absorb the sunlight evenly. Plants lean toward the strongest light.

Ailing houseplants—'They'll reflect all the love you give them'

- Your houseplant will come out of its slump if you cover it with a plastic bag, along with a pest strip. Make sure the entire plant is under the bag. Remove the bag in a few days and you will find it in good health. This is excellent to do when transferring plants from outside into the house.

- Or, feed your plant a tablespoon of castor oil, followed by a good drink of water.

Bug beaters

- *Aphids & Spiders:* Wash the entire plant with mild detergent and water.
- *Black flies:* Combine 2 tablespoons of plain ammonia and 1 quart of water. Water soil.
- *White flies:* Mix 2 tablespoons of dishwashing liquid in 1 gallon of water and spray on leaves.
- *Scales:* For instant removal of slugs, place plant in pot of water.
- *Pests of all kinds:* Plant a garlic clove along with your plant. As it grows, simply keep cutting it down so it will not disturb the appearance of the plant. Garlic will not harm the plant, but the bugs hate it.

House plant on the mend

- A tiny splint made of toothpicks and adhesive tape will often save the broken stem of a plant.

Cleaning plant leaves

- Dust with a feather duster.
- Glycerine is one of the best substances to use if you wish to put a gloss on the leaves of your plants. Put a few drops of glycerine on a cloth and swab the leaves with it. It is much better than olive oil or mayonnaise, since it is not a dust collector.
- A half-and-half mixture of milk and water also makes a fine solution for glossing leaves.

Homemade trellises

- Snip off the hook of a wire coat hanger, bend remaining

wire into a fun, creative shape, such as a heart or a star.
Then, push ends into the pot to make a miniature trellis
for your ivy to grow on.
- Support tall plants with old adjustable brass-like
curtain rods.

Eliminating the scratches
- Corn pads are terrific coasters for plant pots. Simply
stick them on and you will be able to use that pot that
has been scratching your table for years.

Another planting hint
- For good drainage use: broken clay pot, cracked walnut shells, fruit stones, marbles, charcoal or stones on
the bottom of the pots.

Ferns love tea parties too!
- A good tonic for ferns is to water them with weak tea.
In addition to their tea break, plant a wet soggy teabag
along with your fern.
- Let worm-infested ferns meet their 'match'. Stick
matches into the soil with the sulphur end down. For
an ordinary size plant, use 4 matches and for a large
one use 6.
- Ferns enjoy the nitrogen content in a very weak solution of ammonia and water.

Ways to help your cut flowers last longer
- Always cut stems at an angle with a very sharp scissors
or knife.
- Split the ends of thick stems before putting them in a
vase. Split ends give stems a better chance to absorb
moisture.
- Always cut stems under water. That way, no air bubbles can form to stop the free flow of water into the
stem.

- Remove leaves below the waterline, as decaying vegetable matter poisons the water.
- Aspirin tablets, pennies and ice cubes are all said to lengthen the lives of fresh cut flowers. However, the best preservative is 2 tablespoons of white vinegar and 2 tablespoons of cane sugar in a quart of water. The vinegar inhibits the growth of organisms and the sugar serves as food.
- Refrigerate each night. This alone can double their lives.
- Flowers will last longer if not crowded in the vase.

Reviving wilted flowers
- Cut stems and place in hot water. Let them rest in a dark place until water cools. Then, transfer into cold water.

More tips on flowers
- If you have ever smelled a marigold which has been in a vase of water for a few days, you will appreciate this tip. Add a teaspoon of sugar to the water to eliminate the smell.
- Carnations will last longer if placed in water containing a little boric acid.
- Feed geraniums rinsed coffee grounds.
- Place a crushed paper napkin or towel in the bottom of your flower vase if it's too deep for displaying flowers.
- If you have any birth control pills left, dissolve them in water and water violets.
- To add length to short stemmed flowers, slip stems into drinking straws before placing in vase.
- Put a layer of gravel on the top of window boxes to prevent rain from spattering dirt on windows.
- Drop a penny into the vase, so tulips will stand erect and not open too wide.
- To keep water from clouding in a clear vase, add 1 tablespoon of liquid bleach to 1 quart of water.
- Hold long-stemmed flowers erect in a tall wide

mouthed vase by crisscrossing transparent tape across the top.
- Hair rollers tied together and placed at the bottom of a vase make an ideal holder for your arrangement.

Preserving flowers and leaves
- Spray any cut flower with hair spray to make it last longer without shedding. Hold the spray can about a foot away from the bouquet and spray in an upward direction, so as not to cause the flowers to droop.

How to dry flowers
- Mix 10 parts white cornmeal to 3 parts of borax. Bury flowers in the mixture. Leave for 2 weeks and your dried flowers will last for years.
- Another fine preservation method for dried arrangements: First hammer the ends of the branches or the stems of their leaves. Then stand the branches or stem ends in a jar containing a solution of $\frac{2}{3}$ water and $\frac{1}{3}$ glycerine, enough to reach 3 or 4 inches up branches or stems. (You can also lay leaves in the solution.) Allow a week or so for the solution to be absorbed. Some foliage may change colour, but the leaves will last for years.

Food colouring tints flowers
- You can change the colour of cut flowers by mixing food colouring in warm water and placing stems in the solution. The stems absorb the colours and by morning you will see pretty designs and different colours on flowers.

Spring is busting out all over
- In winter when flowers are scarce, go out and prune some twigs or branches of forsythia, crab apples, hawthorn, lilac and other flowering trees and shrubs. Put

122

the stems in a bucket of warm water, then drop in a cottonwool ball saturated with ammonia. Put the pail and branches in a plastic bag and tie securely. Soon the ammonia fumes will force blooms on the branches.

Goodbye to unwanted grass and weeds
- Salted boiling water will immediately kill grass or weeds growing between sections of cement walk.
- To keep grass from growing between bricks in a walk, sprinkle the spaces with salt.

A good deed for your feathered friends . . . They'll love you for it!
- Help make their nesting easier and provide building materials. Collect fluff from your dryer, bits of string, thread from your sewing basket and hair from your brush. Fasten together very lightly and attach to a tree branch.

A 'pine' treat for the birds in the winter
- Cover pine cones with hardened bacon grease or other type of fat. Roll in bird seed or bread crumbs. Hang from a tree branch or tuck into bushes.

More ideas for the birds
- To attract birds to an outdoor birdbath, drop in a few coloured marbles.
- When you cannot find a funnel to put bird seed in the feeder, use the cut-off top of a bleach bottle or an old milk carton.

A perfect seed row marker
- Mark the planting date on each seed packet. Then, slip small plastic bags over each seed packet and secure

with a twist-tie. You will never have doubts about which plants are which if you follow this procedure.

Aid tomato plants with tights
- To avoid cutting into your prize-winning tomato plants, tie the stalks with tights that have been cut lengthwise.

Assuring baby tomatoes a good start
- Mix fireplace ashes into the surrounding soil. Remove the top and bottom lids from largish tins and set a tin over each plant. (Step firmly on the tin to set it into the ground.) Remove tins when plants are a few weeks old.

The know-hows of organic gardening
- Herbs are nature's insecticides. Include a variety of them in your garden.
- Basil near tomatoes repels worms and flies.
- Mint, sage, dill and thyme protect cabbage, cauliflower, broccoli and Brussels sprouts from the cabbage moth.
- Onions and garlic protect your plants from carrot flies, and aphids on lettuce and beans. Onions should be planted near carrots and beets.
- Anise and coriander discourage aphids.
- Radishes planted near cabbage repels maggots.
- Do not plant garlic near peas, nor cabbage near strawberries. They do not like each other.
- Rabbits hate talcum powder. Just dust a little on or around the plants. It also works like a charm in repelling flea beetles. When the rain washes it away, apply more.
- Dried coffee grounds add acid to the soil.
- Soapsuds are a fantastic insecticide. Spray them on liberally.
- Compost piles are important. They are a must for the organic gardener.
- Make an additional fence around your garden with a

row of vegetables. The roots secrete oil which many pests refuse to cross.

- Toss crushed-up egg shells on your garden for plant growth.
- For a quick end to ants, pour boiling water on each ant nest.
- Scatter mothballs around your garden to discourage rabbits and other pests from feasting.

That's all 'fern' now!

the BEST
of hints for
SEWING

An easy way to hem a dress

- A sink plunger is a handy gadget to use when marking a skirt for hemming. Mark the handle at the desired length, then move the plunger around the hem. It stands by itself, leaving your hands free to mark or pin.

Threading a needle

- Spray a bit of hair spray or spray starch on your finger when threading a needle and apply it to the end of the thread. The thread stiffens just enough to ease the job of finding the eye.

Sharpening a machine needle

- Stitch through a piece of sandpaper.

Make heavy seams 'seam' easy

- Rub seams with a piece of hard bar soap. The machine needle will go through the material with ease.

Storage for sewing tools

- Use an empty thermometer case as a holder for extra long and fine needles that are hard to store in a sewing box.
- Use plastic pill bottles with snap-on tops to hold the extra small buttons.

Pins and needles all over the place

- Safety pins can be gathered and threaded on to a pipe

cleaner. Then, bend the pipe cleaner into a circle and twist the ends together.

- Keep a small magnet in your sewing basket and use it to pick up pins and needles that drop to the floor while you are sewing.

Reusing a zipper

- Spray it heavily with spray starch and it will sew like new. Zippo! It works.

Buttons and buttonholes

- Here's a tip for keeping those four-hole buttons on longer. Sew through only two holes at a time, breaking the thread and knotting it for each pair of holes. This way, should one set break loose, the other side will still hold the button.
- Use dental floss or elastic thread to sew buttons on children's clothing. The buttons will take a lot of wear before falling off.
- If you have trouble removing a button from a garment, slide a comb under the button and cut between comb and button with a razor blade.
- To make a straight cut for a buttonhole on heavy fabric, lay buttonhole section over a bar of soap and cut with a razor blade.

A red hot idea for belt holes

- Poke with a red-hot steel knitting needle.

'Snappy' ideas

- Sew the snap point on first. Then take a piece of chalk and touch this little point. Turn the material over, rub it with your finger, and you will find that you have marked the exact place where the snap should be sewed on.

A quick trick for sewing on emblems
- Use a few dabs of any good white glue on the back of the emblem and press it in position on the clothing, then leave it for a few minutes. The emblem can then be stitched by hand or machine without any worry that it will turn out lopsided. The glue subsequently washes out.

Creeping machine foot pedal
- Glue a piece of foam rubber to the bottom of a portable sewing machine foot control and it will not creep on the floor.

Worn elastic
- Whenever elastic that is sewed on a garment becomes worn or stretched, just tack cord elastic through the worn elastic. Pull it up and knot.

Eliminating the knot
- When sewing with a single thread, does it constantly knot? If so, try this: After you thread the needle, be sure to knot the end that was cut off closest to the spool.

After oiling the sewing machine
- Stitch through a blotter several times to avoid surplus oil from damaging your fabrics.

'Darn it'—Two different ways
- Use a glass marble as a darning egg when mending fingers of a glove.
- One of the easiest ways to mend a hole in a garment is to place a thin sheet of paper under the hole and darn back and forth with the sewing machine. When the garment is washed the paper will dissolve. This is ideal for bedsheets with big tears or rips.

A handy pin cushion
- A bar of soap makes an ideal place to stick needles and pins. It lubricates them so that they will go through stiff fabrics with ease.

Great balls of yarn
- When you are working with more than one ball of knitting yarn, put the balls in a plastic bag with small holes, like the bag potatoes come in. Thread the different yarns through various holes in the bag. The yarn will stay clean and untangled throughout the project.

Sewing on plastic
- Put wax paper over the seam and the sewing machine will not stick to the plastic nor pucker. The wax paper will tear off easily after the job is done.

Avoiding the slips and slides when sewing on nylon
- When repairing seams on nylon jackets or lingerie, make the job a lot simpler by placing a piece of paper

underneath the section you are going to sew. Stitch through the fabric and paper. When finished, tear the paper off.

How to make your patterns last longer
- Spray a new pattern with fabric protector. The pattern will last longer, rip less easily and resist wrinkles.

the BEST of hints for
STORING/ SAVING/ SENDING

Damp cupboards

- To help prevent dampness in a cupboard, fill a plastic-lidded coffee tin with charcoal briquets. Punch holes in the cover and place the container on the floor. For larger cupboards use several large tins.
- You can also cut down on dampness by wrapping and tying together 12 pieces of chalk and hanging them in your cupboard.

Musty smells

- For sweet smelling clothes cupboards, hang up an old nylon stocking filled with cedar chips. This also serves as an excellent moth repellant.
- To remove musty odours from a trunk, place a tin filled with cat litter deodoriser inside the trunk overnight.

Helping prevent moth damage

- In addition to mothballs, put whole cloves in pockets of woollen coats or in bags with sweaters when storing for the off season. They help prevent moth damage and have a nice spicy scent.
- Before storing blankets for the summer, wash them and add 2 cups of mothballs to the rinse water.

This hint 'can' solve your problem

- Store out-of-season clothes in large plastic-lidded dust bins. Not only will your clothes be mothproof, they will stay dry in damp cupboards or attics.

Storing fine china plates
- Insert paper plates or paper napkins between fine china plates as you stack to prevent scratching.

Before applying contact paper
- Make patterns of the shelves and drawers with newspaper. Transfer the patterns to the contact paper before cutting and you will have an excellent fit.

Tips for storing jewellery, belts and handbags
- Egg cartons serve as excellent storage containers for jewellery.
- Place a piece of chalk in your jewellery box to prevent costume jewellery from tarnishing.
- To avoid tangled chains and necklaces, screw cup hooks to the inside of your wardrobe door for tangle-free hanging.
- Hook large shower curtain hooks over the clothes rod for hanging handbags and belts.

No spills
- Tack a piece of sewing elastic across the inside of a drawer to keep small bottles (nail polish, ink . . .) upright in your desk or dressing-table drawers.

How to preserve a favourite newspaper cutting
- Dissolve a milk of magnesia tablet in a quart of soda water overnight. Pour into a dish large enough to accommodate the flattened newspaper. Soak cutting for one hour, remove and pat dry. Do not move until completely dry. Estimated life: 200 years.

Wrapping packages
- To premeasure the length of gift wrapping paper from

a large roll, wrap a string around the package first, then cut off the desired length and use it as a measuring guide.

- Before tying a package for posting, wet the string or cord with water. This method prevents the string from slipping, and when dry it will hold extra tight.

Here's more

- Keep clear plastic wrap in the refrigerator to prevent it from ever sticking together.
- Sometimes mildew can be removed from papers and book pages by a good dusting with cornflour. Allow the powder to remain on for several days before giving it the brush-off.
- Your favourite photo negatives can be stored behind the actual print in your album for safekeeping.
- Empty soft-drink cartons are ideal for storing light bulbs.
- When postage stamps are stuck together, place them in the freezer. They will usually come apart and the glue will still be usable.
- Extension cords can be conveniently stored without tangling, by simply winding the cord loosely and slipping it into a cardboard tube (from paper towels or toilet paper).

the BEST of hints for
WALLPAPER/
WOODWORK

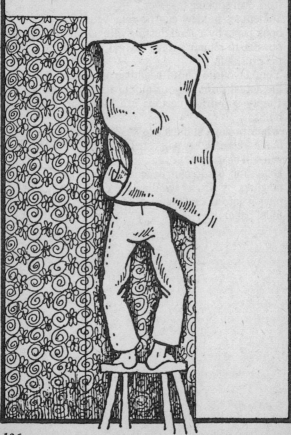

Removing wallpaper

- Use equal parts of vinegar and hot water. Dip roller or sponge into solution and wet paper thoroughly. After two applications the paper should peel off in sheets. Note: Use a paint roller. It is much more effective than using a brush.

Before repapering a wall

- Cover all grease spots with *shellac* and allow to dry thoroughly. This effectively prevents the grease spots from coming through on the new paper.

How much wallpaper?

- Try this formula to determine how many rolls of wall-paper will be needed to paper a room. Multiply the distance around the room (in feet) by the height of the room, then divide by 30. Deduct 2 rolls for every ordinary-sized opening such as windows and doors. The answer will equal the number of rolls needed. This allows for matching patterns.

Wallpapering the bathroom or kitchen

- After papering steamy rooms, paint all joints with clear varnish to prevent peeling.

A quick way to replace vinyl wallpaper

- When taking down the old paper, number each strip from left to right or vice versa. When cutting the new paper, use the numbered strips as a pattern. However, make sure the old and new papers are of the same width. You will save yourself a lot of measuring time with this method.

Patching wallpaper
- When you are tearing (never cut) wallpaper to make a patch, tear towards the wrong side of the paper. The patch will be almost invisible.

Removing unsightly bulges
- Slit the bulge with a razor blade. Using a knife, insert some paste under the paper. Smooth with a wet sponge.

Grease spots on wallpaper
- Make a paste of cornflour and water. Let it remain on the spot until dry, then brush off. If the stain persists, try, try again.
- If the above method fails, try a paste of Fuller's Earth and carbon tetrachloride and use it in the same way.
- Or, apply a piece of clean blotting paper to the grease spot and press with a warm iron. Do more than once, using a fresh blotter each time. Remove any lingering traces by rubbing with a cloth dipped in borax.

Removing crayon marks
- Treat as a greasy crayon.
- Rub lightly with a dry soap-filled steel wool pad. Do not wet.
- Or, rub very gently with bicarbonate of soda sprinkled on a damp cloth.
- Crayon marks on vinyl can be removed with silver polish.

To remove everyday smudges
- Erase away light marks (pencil, fingerprints, dirt) with artgum squares (available at stationers).

Removing cellophane tape
- Put a blotter against the tape and press with a warm iron.

An easy tip to avoid expensive plastering bills
- If the plaster is cracking on the ceiling, try this: Mix some paperwork glue or gum with bicarbonate of soda, making a paste. Apply to cracks with fingers. If the ceiling is coloured, add food colouring to match. This trick could help postpone replastering for months.

Plaster with no lumps
- If you add plaster to water, instead of water to plaster, the mixture will be lump free.

Another plaster tip
- You can slow the hardening of plaster by adding a little vinegar to the mixture.

Cleaning rough plastered walls
- Instead of using a cloth or sponge, try using nylon or Banlon socks. No small pieces will be left behind as you work.

A crack filler
- Fill cracks with steel wool or newspaper before finishing off with plaster.

The best wall cleaner
- Combine $\frac{1}{2}$ cup ammonia, $\frac{1}{4}$ cup white vinegar, $\frac{1}{4}$ cup washing soda and 1 gallon warm water for the perfect solution for cleaning walls.

How to hide nail holes from the landlady

- Rub toothpaste into the hole and smooth with a damp sponge.

Brushing away cobwebs

- Slip a sock or two over the end of a ruler. Secure with a rubber band. Also good for cleaning under the refrigerator and radiators.

the BEST of hints for
WINDOWS

Take the 'pane' out of washing your windows

- Never wash windows on sunny days. They will dry too fast and show streaks.
- Never use soap.
- Add ½ cup ammonia, ½ cup white vinegar and 2 tablespoons of cornflour to a bucket of warm water for a perfect window washing solution.
- For fast clean-ups, wash with a cloth soaked in white vinegar. This method is great when washing only a few indoor windows.
- Shine with newspaper instead of paper towels. It is cheaper and some feel easier. Be sure you have read the papers or the project could take all day.
- No more guess work if you dry the inside panes with vertical strokes and the outside panes with horizontal strokes, or vice versa – you will notice quickly which side has the smudges.
- After windows have dried, rub a clean blackboard eraser over them for a really fine shine.

Before washing the inside windows

- To avoid taking down curtains, drape them through a coathanger and hang from the curtain rod. The curtains will be safely out of the way.

Keeping Jack Frost off windows

- The problem of ice-covered windows can be solved by adding ½ cup surgical spirit or anti-freeze to each quart of water used.
- Rub the inside of windows with a sponge that has been dipped in surgical spirit or anti-freeze. Polish with paper towels or newspaper.
- Try a cloth moistened with glycerine, rub on, leaving

a little of the glycerine on the inside of the glass.
- Or, head south.

Window and mirror cleaner
- Duplicate the 'blue kind' by filling a spray bottle with 3 tablespoons of ammonia, 1 tablespoon vinegar and cool water. Add a drop or two of food colouring.

Spotted window sills
- Pour a little diluted surgical spirit on a soft cloth and rub the entire surface. The spots will not only disappear, but the sills will look freshly painted.

Some rather 'shady' ideas
- Rub unwashable window blinds with a rough flannel cloth which has been dipped in flour.
- A soft eraser may remove spots and stains.
- Keep parchment shades clean by waxing them.

Are your tiebacks straight?
- A foolproof way to get tiebacks straight across from each other when hanging curtains is to use your window blind as a measuring guide.

Window blind tears
- Repair with colourless nail polish. This works wonders on small tears.

Cleaning sliding door tracks
- Generally, the tracks of sliding glass doors are very hard to clean. Try wrapping a small cloth around an eraser and rub dirt away.

Cleaning aluminium window frames
- Try a cream silver polish.

Venetian blinds
- To repair a venetian blind tape that has broken, simply tape the side that faces the wall with heavy duty packing tape. Apply white canvas shoe polish.
- To brighten up the tapes on your blinds, simply rub in white shoe polish with a damp sponge.
- You can quickly clean venetian blinds by saturating a cloth with surgical spirit and wrapping around a rubber spatula. It will easily reach into the tiny slats.

Eliminating sticky windows
- Once a year, dip a small brush in petroleum jelly and paint it on the inside moulding.
- If it is stuck, the divider is probably bent. To fix easily rap the divider to one side.
- Sometimes a vigorous snap to the window rope or chain will do the trick.

Replacing a pane of glass
- To loosen the old pane of glass, pass a red-hot poker slowly over the old putty.

Cheap curtain hem weights
- Use old door keys.

Easy moving curtain rods
- After washing curtain rods, wax them. They will move much better. This applies to new rods as well.

Inserting curtain hooks
- A soap coating will make curtain hooks much easier to push into the fabric.

More hints to remember

More hints to remember

More hints to remember

More hints to remember

More hints to remember

More hints to remember

More hints to remember

More hints to remember

INDEX

155

NEL BESTSELLERS

T037061	BLOOD AND MONEY	*Thomas Thompson*	£1.50
T045692	THE BLACK HOLE	*Alan Dean Foster*	95p
T049817	MEMORIES OF ANOTHER DAY	*Harold Robbins*	£1.95
T049701	THE DARK	*James Herbert*	£1.50
T045528	THE STAND	*Stephen King*	£1.75
T065475	I BOUGHT A MOUNTAIN	*Thomas Firbank*	£1.50
T050203	IN THE TEETH OF THE EVIDENCE	*Dorothy L. Sayers*	£1.25
T050777	STRANGER IN A STRANGE LAND	*Robert Heinlein*	£1.75
T050807	79 PARK AVENUE	*Harold Robbins*	£1.75
T042308	DUNE	*Frank Herbert*	£1.50
T045137	THE MOON IS A HARSH MISTRESS	*Robert Heinlein*	£1.25
T050149	THE INHERITORS	*Harold Robbins*	£1.75
T049620	RICH MAN, POOR MAN	*Irwin Shaw*	£1.60
T046710	EDGE 36: TOWN ON TRIAL	*George G. Gilman*	£1.00
T037541	DEVIL'S GUARD	*Robert Elford*	£1.25
T050629	THE RATS	*James Herbert*	£1.25
T050874	CARRIE	*Stephen King*	£1.50
T050610	THE FOG	*James Herbert*	£1.25
T041867	THE MIXED BLESSING	*Helen Van Slyke*	£1.50
T038629	THIN AIR	*Simpson & Burger*	95p
T038602	THE APOCALYPSE	*Jeffrey Konvitz*	95p
T046850	WEB OF EVERYWHERE	*John Brunner*	85p

NEL P.O. BOX 11, FALMOUTH TR10 9EN, CORNWALL

Postage charge:

U.K. Customers. Please allow 40p for the first book, 18p for the second book, 13p for each additional book ordered, to a maximum charge of £1.49, in addition to cover price.

B.F.P.O. & Eire. Please allow 40p for the first book, 18p for the second book, 13p per copy for the next 7 books, thereafter 7p per book, in addition to cover price.

Overseas Customers. Please allow 60p for the first book plus 18p per copy for each additional book, in addition to cover price.

Please send cheque or postal order (no currency).

Name ....

Address ....

....

Title ....

While every effort is made to keep prices steady, it is sometimes necessary to increase prices at short notice. New English Library reserve the right to show on covers and charge new retail prices which may differ from those advertised in the text or elsewhere.(5)